Endorsements

I have known Patti for several years and I have watched this woman of God grow into a powerful influence for good. Patti and her husband Joe live quiet and peaceable lives. They are a great team and amazing stewards of their time, talent and treasure. *Moving into Abundance* is not just another story, it is a real life; a life which has been infused with grace. Patti's life and story gives hope, perspective and inspiration to millions of people who find themselves in the crosshairs of life. Her resilient faith is worthy of studying and gleaning from. Her trials and triumphs have blessed many people and I am fortunate to be one of those who have been blessed by her leadership. I encourage you to open this book and engage with an open heart. I encourage you to read this with understanding, God is no respecter of persons. What He has done for Patti, He can and will do for you!

—Pastor Shawn Baker, New Life Church in Santa Rosa Beach, Florida, and author of *The Law of Faith: Operating on the Frequency of Heaven*

Move Into Abundance is a powerful debut that follows a young woman who marries her first love—a handsome

Navy SEAL—and then must navigate the uncertainty, fear, and silent sacrifice of raising two children while never knowing where he is or if he is safe. Patti Oliver shares her story with honesty, grit, and deep faith.

This book is more than her journey; it's a testimony of how God meets us in our darkest hours and leads us from scarcity into abundance—emotionally, spiritually, and practically. Readers will be moved by her story and inspired by her growth. You'll walk away encouraged, empowered, and reminded that no season is too broken for God to transform.

— **Missy Maxwell Worton, Award-winning Author of *Don't Mess With This Mama* and CEO & Founder of Warrior Writers Training**

MOVE INTO ABUNDANCE

Survival Lessons of a Navy SEAL Wife

by

PATTI OLIVER

Move into Abundance: Survival Lessons of a Navy SEAL Wife ©2025 Patti Oliver

ISBNs: Paperback 978-1-969202-17-9; e-book 978-1-969202-18-6; Hardback 978-1-969202-19-3

Editor: Donna Bess
Cover Design: Atindra Nath
Publisher: Light Warrior Publishing

Editorial liberties: Names of God and references to Him are capitalized, and satan and the enemy are lowercased.

Disclaimer: The conversations in this book all come from the author's recollections. They are not written to represent word-for-word transcripts. Rather, the author has retold them in a way that evokes the feeling and meaning of what was said. In all instances, the essence of the dialogue is a close and accurate account of what took place. The author has changed the names of several individuals and places and may have changed some identifying characteristics and details for the protection of many in this book.

To my children—Alison, Brandon, Krista, and Ryan. And to my late husband Doug, their father. Every day for thirty years held a new adventure. Sowing into their lives has brought me a harvest of love, joy, and encouragement beyond measure.

To Joe Oliver, my love, my best friend. After twelve years of widowhood, God renewed His promise to me through you. Thank you for blessing my life with your presence and unwavering support.

"Delight yourself also in the Lord, and He shall give you the desires of your heart. Commit your way to the Lord, trust also in Him, and He shall bring it to pass."
(Psalm 37:4-5 NKJV)

The Invitation

Did you know that God wants every part of you to flourish? God's heart for you is abundance—not just in finances, but in peace, purpose, wholeness, health, and wisdom. It's a life where your soul can breathe, your spirit can soar, and your body can thrive.

That doesn't mean life is always easy. Mine hasn't been. But along the way, I learned to walk with God through the everyday moments, the broken places, and the unexpected blessings.

In this book, I'll share stories, lessons, and truths that have changed me—truths that might shift something in you, too. These pages are an invitation to reflect, reset, and reclaim what's already been promised to you by a God who loves you more than you can imagine.

"Now to Him who is able to do exceedingly abundantly above all that we ask or think, according to the power that works in us."
Ephesians 3:20 NKJV

Lean in and journey with me as I learn who God is, who I am in Him, and what it truly means to live an abundant life. It's the journey of a lifetime. And as you turn these pages, I pray you begin to see just how possible this abundant life can be for you.

~Patti Oliver

TABLE OF CONTENTS

Chapter 1

I've Always Been a Dreamer

*"Go confidently in the direction of your dreams.
Live the life you have imagined."*
—Henry David Thoreau

I WAS THIRTEEN when wandering the Ocean City boardwalk became my escape. Salt air in my lungs, the roar of waves in my ears, and—for the first time in a long time—no one telling me who to be.

For a few wonderful hours, I belonged to no one but myself.

I wandered past candy shops and beachside boutiques; the scent of buttered popcorn and saltwater taffy carried on the breeze. Red candy apples gleamed in the windows like treasure, calling my name. But what drew me most were the rows and rows of posters—each one stamped with a quote or affirmation that felt like water to my thirsty soul. I scribbled my favorites in a little notebook I carried everywhere.

I didn't know it then, but I was already just trying to survive. I was the girl who smiled on the outside and cried behind closed doors. The one who absorbed every jab and criticism, with every word a reminder that I wasn't enough. But dared to believe otherwise.

That notebook became my lifeline. Each quote was a stepping stone. Each affirmation was a flicker of hope. They were creating resilience.

And somehow it worked.

I started college with big-city dreams: buyer meetings, fashion shows, with lots of glorious runways. I wanted to become a buyer, maybe even a designer.

Near the end of my first semester, my advisors arranged behind-the-scenes tours of Macy's, Saks Fifth Avenue, and Lord & Taylor in New York City. I was still in my teens and suddenly backstage in the world I had only seen in glossy magazines. I couldn't explain it at the time, but something in me came alive. It wasn't just curiosity—it felt like a calling. I saw myself living this life.

I remember the professionals saying, "You don't necessarily need a college degree. You can work your way up from the bottom."

Those words stuck.

Soon after, I wrote to the owner of the boutique I had worked at in high school. I boldly asked him if he'd consider me for a buying position. He remembered me. He said he appreciated my work ethic, and so he created a new role just for me.

At eighteen, I became the buyer for the accessories department and assistant buyer for lingerie at Deb and Joy Shops—a growing chain with thirty locations. Just four years after scribbling "I was made for more" in my notebook, I was living it out in Philadelphia.

I was soaring.

Every week, my boss and I took the train to Manhattan's garment district. The streets of New York pulsed with energy. The clackety-clack of rolling clothing racks felt like music to my ears. Steam hissed from manholes and vents, where snowmelt met the city's underground arteries. It was loud and electric, but I loved every second of it.

Vendors schmoozed with offers of food, samples, and coffee. I'll never forget the Jewish owner at Sarne Bags asking me in her thick New York accent, "Do you want a pastrami on rye?"

One morning, just before stepping out of the train onto the platform, he looked at me and said, "You need to grow up fast. You're now dealing with serious professionals. Watch closely. Learn. And be very wise."

He was right. We were spending tens of thousands of dollars.

On one of my first solo trips, I weighed barely one hundred pounds, but I was making $30,000 in purchasing decisions. The creaky elevator groaned as I stepped out onto the twentieth floor of a high-rise showroom. My stomach twisted with excitement and fear. I felt like a big deal, and my boss expected that I perform like one. It was a rush.

I felt alive. I felt important. For eighteen months, I reveled in the hustle and heartbeat of the city. I had worked hard for this life. And I was proud of myself.

But slowly, the glamour began to dull.

Seventy-hour workweeks and long commutes through bitter Philly snow. Not to mention the constant pressure to perform. I was twenty years old and already burning out.

I admit, once I recognized my sadness, the decision was easy. One day, I quit. I needed rest.

I packed up my car and drove south to North Carolina at my parents' invitation. I had no plan— just the desperate need for warmth, a simpler life, and some space to breathe.

I took a job as an assistant manager at a discount retail chain—nothing like the designer showrooms of Manhattan. But it was stable and definitely more manageable. And for the first time in a long while, I could have a life.

I moved into a tiny second-floor apartment— just me and the world. An interior designer friend helped me arrange my mismatched furniture, transforming my space from chaotic to charming. I was content.

And for the first time in nearly two years, I exhaled.

In the quiet of those evenings, I began to dream again. I clipped magazine articles, beauty tips, travel destinations, and things I wanted to do. I journaled my prayers, leaving pieces of myself on each page.

But something was shifting.

I no longer prayed for success—I prayed for meaning.

I prayed for:

- A husband who shared my love of the outdoors.

- Adventure.
- Always living close to the ocean.
- A partner who wouldn't just fill the space beside me—but walk with me.

I didn't know it then, but those prayers were preparing my heart for a new kind of dream. One that wouldn't sparkle on a runway or fit the streets of Manhattan—but would allow my heart to sparkle.

I went to church early one Sunday morning and prayed for the man of my dreams. "Lord, let me meet the man you have for me, doing what I love to do." I left that altar with expectation.

That same morning, I set out for a solo skiing adventure. I left my home in Charlotte, NC, and headed to Beech Mountain, where I would stay at my friend's condo on the slope. The three-hour drive was easy until I hit the narrow, curvy mountain roads. That didn't stop me; I was twenty years old and excited about the trip. I swatted away my fears of being alone.

7

When I arrived, I went straight to the slopes. The view from the chairlift was breathtaking as I rode to the top. The air was clean, crisp, and cold. My many layers of clothing kept my core warm. As I hovered above, I loved watching the skier's race down the slope.

My eyes caught a handsome, clean-cut man skiing back and forth with such style and grace. I hoped I would run into him at some point on the slopes. On my next ride up the chair lift, I was searching for that hunk. There he was again. He looked beautiful from so far away. The third time up, I did not see him.

As I skied down the slope, my eyes spotted him resting on his ski poles. I knew this was my opportunity to talk to him. I was nervous, yet bold, and not intimidated to strike up a conversation with strangers. My time working in Philadelphia and New York City gave me the confidence to talk to all kinds of people. Surely, I could talk to this guy!

I had no reserves. I skied right up to him and told him I enjoyed watching him ski. When he looked at me, his smile warmed my heart, and it felt like his piercing blue eyes looked into my soul. As we talked, we had an instant connection. He even knew my small hometown in Pennsylvania, which was so far from where we both were.

We intended to ski the next run together, but we got separated by the ski lift attendant. Then, the chair lift broke, and I was stuck halfway up the mountain for thirty minutes. The wind was blowing, and I became extremely cold. I had been skiing all day with a ski patrol guy I had just met. When the chairlift started again, we were both freezing and went into the ski patrol shack to warm ourselves.

After I sufficiently thawed out, I headed down the slope. My eyes searched for the delish dish—hunk, I mean, the good-looking guy. My heart sank as I realized I had lost him because of the delay. My mind flashed to my daily prayer: "Lord, I know someday I will meet the man of my dreams doing what I love to do." I was disappointed because I thought he might have been the answer to my prayer. Maybe it was not today. Maybe it was not him.

At the end of the day, I was standing by the pro shop waiting to get the key to my friend's condo when I saw him walking down the steps toward me. He greeted me with another beautiful smile. We introduced ourselves and chatted for a while. Doug asked for my phone number, but I asked him to give me his address and number first. I actually wrote him a letter that included my contact information, and he called right away to invite me to visit him in Raleigh.

Five days later, I drove two hours and fifteen minutes to Duke University to meet him. Doug was doing experimental diving at the Hyperbaric Unit at Duke. On our first date, he showed me around the campus; he lived right in the center of the university. That's when he told me he was a Navy SEAL. I did not know what a SEAL was in 1978, and I don't think very many people did. He explained that a SEAL was an elite warrior suited for all aspects of unconventional warfare. He was trained to operate on the sea, air, and land in any weather conditions. His specialty was winter warfare, which was why he was such an excellent skier. I was more impressed as I got to know him.

I was always enthralled with the adventures he had planned for us. Motorcycle rides and picnics in the woods. Pig roast camping trips at the lake. Water skiing and snow skiing. He knew he had met his match when he learned I was scuba-qualified and loved rock climbing. I had my own stories to tell him, like how I reached the end of my rope while rock climbing with fifty feet to land because the rope was too short, and how I got stuck on a ledge and lost in the woods of the very mountains we had been skiing in. I was adventurous before I met him.

A whirlwind romance ensued, and we were engaged in six weeks. We got married one year later with a traditional Polish wedding. The reception included dancing on the tabletops!

Doug planned all aspects of our honeymoon. We took off in a military cargo C-130 plane, which was a very large plane for just the twenty of us. We were given earplugs as we entered the aircraft and sat in cargo seats on our way to our destination of Luquillo Beach, Puerto Rico. There, he rented a condominium, a short walk from the beach. The honeymoon included wonderful excursions of scuba diving, touring, and surf fishing.

On one outing, I asked him, "What are you fishing for, Doug?"

"Barracuda," was his response. I was out of the water so quickly!

"Really? You're baiting Barracuda, and I am swimming here?"

I should have known being married to a SEAL would be more adventurous than I was expecting. We set up our first home in Virginia Beach, Virginia.

Chapter 2
The Choice That Changed Everything

"Out of my struggle comes the strength.
That pressure created diamonds."
—Patti Oliver

THE SUN WAS setting over Virginia Beach Boulevard as I drove home from work, my blonde hair whipping in the wind through the sunroof. I slipped off my suit jacket, shook out my hair, and let the music play loud, classic '80s tunes thumping through the BMW speakers. The scent of ocean salt filled the air, calming my nerves after another high-pressure day.

I shifted gears, both literally and mentally. The drive home was the part of the day I cherished— the transformation from professional woman to mama. As I drove, I glanced down at my wedding ring sparkling in the fading light.

Doug had fallen in love with me from the moment we met. Even now, though I didn't know where he was in the world, I could still feel that love. But it didn't fill the ache of his absence. The quiet loneliness—the kind only military spouses truly understand—settled in again like a familiar shadow.

Still, I focused on gratitude. I had come so far from the scared little girl crying in her bedroom to a woman with a thriving career, a beautiful home, and two wonderful children. Alison, my curly-haired beach baby, was now four, and Brandon, my happy-go-lucky baby boy, just turned one. They were my joy.

With a full heart, I pulled into the driveway. The moment I stepped inside, the giggles and tiny footsteps of my sweet children echoed through the house. Jenny, our exuberant Labrador, barked in circles at my arrival. I kicked my heels off and knelt, trying to listen to their stories without ruining my favorite skirt. My nanny rattled off the day's events before rushing out with her children, as I mentally ran through what I could make for dinner.

I had crafted the life I once dreamed of—thriving children, a home filled with laughter, and a successful career. And yet, something still felt off—subtly unsettling. I couldn't name it then. But I knew it was true.

Nearly a year later, I was driving up the same driveway, but my spirit had that familiar unsettled feeling, as if something was wrong. I opened the front door and was greeted not by laughter, but by my nanny's pale, trembling face.

"There's something wrong with your child," she spouted like a hose under pressure, her voice sharp with panic. I was not quite sure what was happening. But I joined in her panicked response.

"Alison!" she said with a frustrated tone.

"Alison?" My mind raced through every terrifying possible scenario. Illness? An accident? My stomach twisted! But nothing could have prepared me for what she said next.

She continued, "Your daughter locked herself in the room and would not come out. She has covered the entire room in baby powder. Even the ceiling!"

Speechless, I stood frozen, struggling to make sense of her words as I peered past her into the house. Alison sat glued to the TV, and her room still covered with a fog of baby powder. She never said how she got Alison out of the room. Instead, overwhelmed and flustered, my nanny stormed up to me and handed me her keys. "I quit!" she abruptly blurted out as she walked past my still-paralyzed mind out the door.

And just like that, my carefully balanced world began to unravel.

I believed Alison was having fun and playing around, but I also knew something didn't feel right. I didn't know exactly what it was or how to handle it. One concern was that she had not spoken until she was two years and four months old. Typically, girls begin to talk between ten and fourteen months of age. However, shortly after her brother was born, she suddenly started speaking in partial sentences, expressing her thoughts freely. Though I knew this was not typical, I overlooked it since the doctor said little about it.

What was I to do now? I thought. *Why would the nanny, without any explanation, choose to just quit on the spot? Was there something else she wasn't telling me?*

For some people, the baby powder incident may have seemed small, but in my world of delicate emotional balance, it felt more like a straw that broke the camel's back. I sat feeling the weight of the world rest on my shoulders. I wanted my husband.

Married to this SEAL meant I lived two very different lives: one when he was home, and one when he was deployed—a Military term for 'gone on a mission.' I lived life as a single mom most of the time. This time was no different. I was once again thrust to the front of a crisis to manage it alone.

In those early years, Doug and I would talk on the phone once a week for fifteen minutes on a Sunday. With the kids competing to speak to Daddy, there was hardly time to talk about anything else. There were no video calls, text messages, or constant communication like today. International calls were expensive. Each conversation was measured, carefully rationed between updates and emotions. And always, there was the unspoken weight of what he couldn't tell me—where he was, what he was doing, or when he would return.

We lived a life of uncertainty. Even when he was home, the phone could ring and he would leave in the middle of the night, without warning. I never knew where, and I wasn't even sure if he knew. We'd both scan the news, reading between the headlines, trying to guess which part of the world he might have to go to next. The instability of life was relentless, and parenting alone under that kind of pressure was suffocating.

I wouldn't wish this on my worst enemy, I thought.

After the nanny quit, I cycled through three more babysitters in just eight weeks. I could not find anyone to come to my house. I was now forced to drive the children to the sitters. These changes alone added hours of drive time to my daily commute. With each change in sitter, I felt more like a failure because they were not the right fit for my babies.

I loved my children, but I was drowning—working full-time, managing a household, parenting alone, and trying to hold up a fragile image of strength. Inside, I was falling apart. I was truly at my wits' end.

Reflecting on when Doug and I first started dating, Doug said matter-of-factly, "If you can't handle this life, the life of a Navy SEAL wife, you need to get out now."

At the time, I boldly told him, "I can handle it!"

However, after my first disappointment—when he couldn't show up for a date, for reasons unknown to me—I exclaimed in exasperation,

"Nope, this is too hard for me, I am out!" I cried my eyes out for hours, I was brokenhearted with my decision.

And then the phone rang. "Can I come to visit you?" Doug asked in a humble tone.

When he arrived, I discovered he didn't come because he was doing experimental diving for the Navy at Duke University. The divers were used as human guinea pigs, put under pressure to see at what point they'd get the bends—also known as decompression sickness, which occurs when a diver surfaces too quickly after spending time at depth. They were creating new dive charts for a new piece of equipment. On one of those dives, Doug's ear was punctured. Coming to see me on his motorcycle, a two-and-a-half-hour drive, with a hole in his eardrum, was painful.

Yet, there he was, standing in my apartment. I felt ashamed when I found out the reason. Of course, he encouraged me that we could work things out, and I agreed. I changed my mind and decided I could make it through the "alone times" after all.

Now, five years later, I was back to feeling that I couldn't handle my life without him present for our family!

I heard only twelve percent of Navy SEAL marriages last. I thought I would be one who would be lucky enough to beat the odds. Now, I wasn't so sure. But, reminding myself of how much Doug loved me and his children, I determined not to faint but to push onward.

Losing my nanny left me at my wits' end. I needed to figure out how to recover from this. *But how?*

I felt like something was ending—was it my grip on control? My illusion of strength? I could not be sure, but life was surely crumbling. Life felt unmanageable. I never considered the single-parenting aspect of being married to a Navy SEAL.

That night, after tucking the kids into bed and wiping my tears for the hundredth time, I sat on the edge of my bed, completely undone. My career had taken years to build, but now even that felt uncertain. The loneliness, the pressure, the endless juggling—had finally broken me.

What does one do when they are losing control? I did the only thing I knew to do. Like so many other times in my life, when I was in trouble—

I cried out to God. "Lord, help me."

Desperate Prayers

The words came out anxious and raw, barely louder than a quiet groan. But in that whisper was surrender—the kind that comes in desperation. More or less a white flag—"I give up." This surrender was far beyond what I had experienced previously. Every attempt at a decision to move forward left me feeling as if I were being thrust into the rocks by a giant wave, tossing me against my will.

I remembered crying on Rose's shoulder. Rose was a petite, soft-spoken blonde woman of wisdom. She was an older SEAL team wife—calm, steady, and someone I had come to trust. She had mentioned she knew a child development specialist and gently suggested I give her a call.

Searching for answers, I picked up the phone. Though it was late, I thought I would leave a message; to my surprise, Elly answered.

Through sobs of exhaustion and perhaps even fear, I poured out everything—about Alison, about my suspicion since the day she was born that something was not right, since she had a constant need to be held. Her language skills developed late. Alison had a seizure at age three, and she stopped breathing. Thankfully, Doug was home and was able to resuscitate her. She was taken to the hospital by ambulance and given medication so they could do an Electroencephalogram (EEG) to check her brain waves.

The nurse told us, "She was given enough medication to knock out a horse." Yet all that medication didn't affect Alison; our thirty-five-pound child was alert. We left the hospital with more questions than we came with!

Elly listened with a kind, steady voice. She asked questions I hadn't expected—questions that went far beyond Alison. Elly was a military wife and understood the unique pressures that came with the military lifestyle—long deployments and the inability to reach our husbands regularly.

Elly asked insightful questions that prompted me to reflect on my life decisions: "Do you ever wonder if it's time to focus on what should be the most important things, like your husband and children?"

She left a pause in the air, but I could not answer. So many thoughts were going through my mind. *Isn't that exactly what I have been doing? They are fed and clothed, happy, and having fun with a nanny at the house.*

She went on, "Are you feeling a pull to deeper things with more purpose?"

Again, words flooded my mind, but they could not reach my lips. A purpose? I considered, What *does she mean … deeper things?*

As our conversation progressed, her words were awakening my consciousness. I was beginning to understand the deeper meanings and the purpose she was speaking about—things that matter more than a fantastic job and a nanny.

There was a part of me that was craving more balance and peace. Then, the revelation came.

I was thinking, *Wow, she is right. My life is a mess!* I had been seeking a career over family. It was all about me first. *How were my desires not making room for my husband and children?* I had to think about that.

And then, gently but boldly, Elly said something I'll never forget: "I can't help your daughter until I help you."

My walls began to crumble. The deeper our conversation went, the more I realized this wasn't just about my daughter.

Her words felt like a heavy weight on my chest. For a moment, I wondered, *What is wrong with me? I am asking about my daughter.* But then I realized I was a hamster on a wheel that never stopped.

Elly saw what I had been blind to. She pointed out how I was trying to fix everything in my own strength. After all, isn't that the nature of most military women whose husbands are gone? But she helped me see that what I needed most was not to come up with another solution—it was surrender.

She explained that when we have a relationship with the Lord, He intervenes on our behalf, and we can trust Him. God has proved himself faithful as the husband and father I needed during Doug's absence.

As Elly spoke, my heart continued softening. Recognizing the shift, she asked: "Are you ready to let Jesus be Lord of your life?"

Tears came again, but not from distress. This time, they came when I relinquished control. I let go and let God have my life. I had known about Jesus since I was a young girl. I had gone to church. I believed in Him, but I had never let Him truly lead. I was still in control. And control had left me exhausted.

"Yes," I whispered. "Yes, I'm ready."

That night, over the phone, I prayed the prayer that would change everything:

"Dear Lord Jesus, I am a sinner. I repent for my sins. Please forgive me. I believe you died for my sins. I ask you to be the Lord and Savior of my life. I've made a mess of things. I need your help."

As the word "help" left my mouth, I felt peace wrap me like a heavy, warm blanket. I exhaled deeply, like I had been holding my breath for years. In that moment, I felt something I hadn't felt in a very long time: refreshing hope. I felt the richness of His supernatural presence and love surround me like a glove. My circumstances had not changed, but for the first time, I felt a release.

Chapter 3

Learning to Love and Be Loved

"... to know this love that surpasses knowledge ..."
(Ephesians 3:19 NIV)

I BEGAN TO EXPERIENCE something new—a hunger to know more of the Lord. My circumstances had not changed, but I had, and I knew what I had to do. I went into work determined to quit my job. I was taking a leap of faith. I was not afraid, even though I had the car and house payments to consider. I didn't ask Doug for permission; I just knew this was what I needed to do. I was tired of the cutthroat world and extreme pressure to perform.

With an air of confidence and a twinge of fear, I walked into my supervisor's office and handed in my two-week notice. My coworkers laughed, as they were sure I was bluffing. But when my final day came, and my desk was empty, the shock was not only to them, but also to me, as well. The reality of my surrender hit me. I had stepped out of the boat. Now I was walking on water. *God, I trust you.*

Uncertainty crept in silently. I didn't have a plan —just forward motion. Yet, I had peace because I knew I was on a good path to this new life.

You see, I was on a journey to learn to align my desires with God's plan for our lives. He had given me a desire to follow him wholeheartedly. His Spirit came ALIVE within me; there was excitement about what the future would hold.

In this new life as a full-time mom, my everyday stress of crushing deadlines had turned into the simple joys of giggles and no alarm clock. As I woke up in the mornings, I loved lying in bed saying, "Thank you, Jesus, I am out of the rat race." I could slowly breathe in and out, relaxing, looking to Jesus to help me in this journey of motherhood.

It had been three years since I was a full-time mom. That was when I lived in England. I would hop on a double-decker bus, Alison in my arms and a stroller in tow, and we'd go exploring for the day—even though she was a baby. I loved being a stay-at-home mom then and I was excited to be doing it again.

My friend Rose celebrated my decision with me. She also rejoiced in my salvation, along with all the angels in heaven. She had been praying for me. She walked alongside me faithfully and helped guide me as I learned about my new life in Christ. She checked on me daily, sharing Scriptures to encourage and strengthen me. With her gentle voice and deep love for the Lord, she patiently taught me things I'd never fully understood before.

I'll never forget the morning she asked, "Patti, do you know God loves you unconditionally?"

Her words caught me off guard. *Of course, God loves me. Doesn't He love everyone? But unconditionally?* That was harder to accept.

I spent my entire life trying to earn love from my parents, my job, and even in my marriage. I performed to be accepted and behaved to be approved. Love was always measured and always attached to my success or failure. I felt loved when I was obedient and quiet, or when I met my parents' expectations, which I often failed to do.

Yet Rose insisted, "God's love isn't like people's love. He loves you even when you feel unworthy. You don't have to earn it."

That truth has both comforted and challenged me. Part of me wanted to believe it. Part of me couldn't fathom it. I had made numerous mistakes and failed many times. *How could He love this version of me? The flawed version? The angry version? Or the overwhelmed mother who yelled at her kids.* I carried hidden wounds from years of feeling unseen and unheard.

However, God was persistent. His love kept knocking on the door of my heart. Little by little—sometimes seemingly imperceptibly slow, but surely as the sun rises in the mornings—my heart began to open to His unconditional love.

This concept of Him loving me even when I didn't love Him was changing my heart. Yes, God's love was different than man's love. Often, I would have to do a course correction and remind myself that He loved me even when I didn't love myself, and even when I made mistakes. God's love and goodness redeemed me, and they also redeemed my mistakes.

One might have thought that allowing Jesus to love me would be easy. After all, He created me perfectly. But the imperfect version of Patti—the one I saw and felt every day—was ever present in my mind. I struggled to reconcile how someone so Holy could love someone who felt so flawed.

The truth I had to embrace was this:

I could not earn His love.

It was never about performance or perfection.

He loved me simply because He created me.

And though I didn't always see or feel that truth, it remained constant and unchanging.

His warm embrace of love was an experience I had never felt before, and I clung to it tightly. I had to stop my mind from thinking negative thoughts that the devil was sowing.

I would pray out loud: "Lord, expose the root in my heart that causes me to stumble.

Your word says I am worthy; I am loved."

I reflected on the warm hug I felt God gave me, the night I surrendered to Him. I relished the gratitude I had for His love.

He gave His love so freely.

"I am deserving of His love," I blurted out. Once I declared that statement, my mind was flooded with thoughts about His love:

His love draws me.

His love does not condemn.

His love believes the best.

His love hopes all things.

His love endures all things.

His love doesn't keep a record of MY wrongs. Why am I keeping a record of my wrongs, I mused.

God, your love enables me to forgive.

God, if you can forgive me, I can forgive me.

I was allowing that to sink in. I am so blessed to have this new life! God's mercies are new every morning. Help me, Lord, to recognize the lies and combat them with Your love.

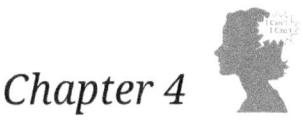

Chapter 4

The Voices That Hold Me Back

"... bringing into captivity every thought to the obedience of Christ."
(2 Corinthians 10:5 KJV)

I YEARNED TO KNOW more about the revelations of this divine life I was living and my identity in Christ. I knew the Bible said the Holy Spirit was alive and working within me. I made up my mind to serve God with tenacity and remain committed. I never wanted to return to the old me.

But beneath the determination was a reality I could not ignore: I was trapped in a cycle I could not escape.

I rehearsed saying, "Forgetting those things which are behind and reaching forward to those things ahead" (Philippians 3:13 NKJV). I was learning to silence those lies with truth. God's Word spoke louder.

"Forgetting" in this verse doesn't mean to erase from your memory. It means to no longer care for it, or to neglect it. It means choosing not to dwell on or be defined by the past. It stops constantly resurfacing in the mind and loses its power over your future.

Forgetting my past wasn't enough—I longed to be free from it. However, true freedom was beyond my own strength. Leaning on God became the only way forward. Time spent with Him, renewing my mind, was reshaping my thinking.

The battle was far from easy. Old habit patterns were hard to break. But very necessary if I were to give way to new, Godly habits. I replaced condemnation with God's promises, fear with faith, and regret with redemption.

What surprised me most about surrender was how much it revealed the broken places inside me. I thought I would feel instantly fixed. Instead, I found myself embroiled in a constant inner battle, years of pain, and self-unforgiveness.

My emotions raged—old triggers, deep insecurities, and patterns I couldn't seem to break. I wanted to respond with grace, but I still often reacted with frustration. The smallest thing—my children arguing, my husband being gone, feeling left behind—would send me into anger, then guilt, then shame.

The same questions kept circling my mind—spinning endlessly, and I felt I wasn't moving forward.

I cried out to God. I repented. A resulting sense of relief would fill me—only to be back in the cycle with the next trigger. My life was on a perpetual loop, like a bad movie.

It felt like I was fighting an invisible enemy that lived inside my head. And in many ways, I was.

From my earliest years, I believed I was bad; everything I did seemed wrong, and my parents always made sure I was corrected for it. The problem wasn't just my behavior—it was the lies I believed. Words from my childhood still echoed in my soul. *You're stupid. You can't do anything right. You're too emotional. You're a disappointment.* Those became my inner soundtrack, and satan was happy to keep playing it.

Lies overshadowed all my life decisions. I carried the weight of my mistakes like a ball and chain. I remember wondering, *Why do I keep doing these things?*

Dr. Caroline Leaf, a scientist, says that if you believe you can't, you truly can't. She explains in her video, *Who Switched Off My Brain?* Negative thoughts cause the brain to release chemicals that block your ability to process and perform.

I had to stop the negative thinking. So, when the lie came in, "*God can't fix me. I'm unlovable.*" I combat it with the truth—"*God can and will fix me because He loves me.*"

Oh, how I tried, in my own strength, to stop doing what displeased God. But I would lose my temper, repent sincerely, try harder, and fail again. Each time, guilt returned like a storm, wrapping me in despair and hopelessness. I hated myself for it.

Then I found in Romans 7 of the Bible that Paul understood my struggle.

"I do not understand what I do. For what I want to do I do not do, but what I hate I do."
(Romans 7:15 NIV)

Paul's words felt like my own journal. He went on to say in verse 19, "I keep doing the evil I do not want to do."

Everything started to make sense: I couldn't fix myself. And that realization terrified me—until I read Romans 8:1 (NIV):

"Therefore, there is now no condemnation for those who are in Christ Jesus."

God wasn't condemning me—He was seeing me through Jesus. Still, the battle inside raged. My mind had been shaped by the negative, limiting words spoken over me. They became a stronghold, I believed, was the truth.

The Cycle I Faced:

1. Get angry
2. Repent sincerely
3. Fall into despair ("I can't stop this")
4. Try to be "good" for a time
5. Get triggered, and start the process all over again

The devil would whisper reminders of my past, even during my best days. Deep down, I wanted to respond with love and kindness, not frustration. But I didn't know how to uproot the lies. So, I began declaring..."*Nothing—absolutely nothing—is too difficult for You, God...not even me!*" (Luke 1:37, paraphrased).

Eventually, the time came when I was able to name the voices holding me back—the lies telling me who I was. But knowing that those were simply lies wasn't enough. I had to learn to replace the lies with God's truth.

Chapter 5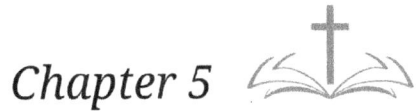
My True Identity in Him

"If you confess with your mouth the Lord Jesus and believe in your heart that God raised Him from the dead, you will be saved."
(Romans 10:9 NKJV)

THE SCRIPTURE ABOVE became a starting point for me. My part was to speak and believe what the Word of God says. That's faith in action.

Once again, I would say to myself, "Patti, out with the old, in with the new!" I knew I had to press in to receive the fullness of all God had for me.

I learned that transformation is not about trying harder; it's about thinking differently. I began to recognize foundational truths, such as:

* I was created in the image of God
* I am spirit, soul, and body.
* My soul is my mind, will, and emotions.
* My spirit is alive in Christ.

I rehearsed truths from His Word like, "And I am sure of this, that he who began a good work in you will bring it to completion at the day of Jesus Christ" (Philippians 1:6 ESV). I also had the tenacity to press into the fullness of all that God had for me.

Now:

- I know His Spirit
- I know He helps me.
- I know His Grace changes me.

Therefore:

- I know God will fix what concerns me.
- I know He can—and He will.
- I know I don't understand how, but I know He will.

He's a creative God, and He creates what is best for me. That's my belief. I can't tell God how to work that miracle out for me. I now take on His thoughts, but through His grace.

> *"For his ways are higher than my ways and his thoughts are higher than my thoughts."*
> **(Isaiah 55:9 NKJV)**

Still, my efforts were not helping as much as I had hoped. One breaking point—and yes, there were many—came when my husband returned from deployment and casually announced another trip—without me. Without us!

I snapped.

I slammed my fist into the kitchen wall and left a gaping hole! I hated what I had done. I immediately repented, but the hole mocked me every time I saw it. I felt condemned and ashamed that my emotions could be so out of control.

But from that incident, God showed me that my emotions weren't the enemy. Rather, it was my agreement with the lies that I had believed.

Renewing your mind involves changing your thoughts to move beyond old ways of thinking and embracing a new pattern of belief. Joyce Meyer says in her book, *The Battlefield of the Mind,* that we deal with "stinking thinking" when we have habitual negative ways of thinking that can stop progress in areas of faith, relationships, and personal growth.

Most have heard the definition of insanity—frequently attributed to Albert Einstein or Benjamin Franklin—as "doing the same thing over and over and expecting different results."[1] I realized I had been living this roller coaster of anger and its cycle for far too long.

I had been driven by fear, performance, and perfectionism. So, I began a deliberate process of renewing my mind each time I was triggered, and I chose to:

1. **Identify the lie I was believing.**
   - *Example:* "I'm too broken for God to fix me. I'm unlovable."

2. **Replace the lie with truth from God's Word.**
   - *Example:* "I am loved with an everlasting love" (Jeremiah 31:3, paraphrased)

3. **Repeat it until I believe it (Using a multi-sensory approach):**

   - **Writing** Scripture in my journal.

   - **Speaking** them out loud

   - **Hearing** them over and over.

"Faith comes by hearing, and hearing by the Word of God," according to the Bible.

Over time, those truths moved from my head into my heart. I began to see progress—not because I had mastered self-control, but because grace was doing in me what I could not do for myself.

The woman I had been was slowly fading, and in her place was emerging a woman who was learning to rest in the love of her Heavenly Father.

I was finally discovering my true identity:

I am perfectly imperfect Patti and perfectly loved by God!

Chapter 6

The Abundant Truth About Who I Am

"I have come that they may have life, and that they may have it more abundantly."
(John 10:10 NKJV)

KNOWING WHAT NEEDED to change was only half the battle. I could see the broken patterns clearly, but awareness without transformation became its own prison of shame and guilt. What was needed was not another self-improvement plan. I needed a complete identity shift.

His promises had to be my foundation…not my past. I had to stop replaying my failures like a highlight reel and start anchoring my mind to what God says about me.

My daily call to action became my life verse.

> *"Do not conform to the pattern of this world but be transformed by the renewing of your mind."*
> **(Romans 12:2 NIV)**

Renewing my mind was not a one-time event—it was a daily choice, a continual and intentional process of choosing truth over lies. But somewhere along the way, that choice became less of a battle. Don't get me wrong, I still struggled. But I was having more victories over the negative thinking.

Who I am in Christ

This list was a tool I used to help me declare His truth over my life. (All Scripture in this section is paraphrased.)

- I am loved with an everlasting love (Jeremiah 31:3).
- I am chosen and appointed to bear fruit (John 15:16).
- I am created in the image of God (Genesis 1:27).
- I am three parts: spirit, soul, and body (1 Thessalonians 5:23).

* I am redeemed and forgiven (Ephesians 1:7).
* I am a new creation; the old has gone, the new is here (2 Corinthians 5:17).
* I am fearfully and wonderfully made (Psalm 139:14).
* I am a child of the King (Romans 8:16-17).
* I am no longer defined by the sin that dwells in me (Romans 7:20).

I now live from a place of security, not striving.

Additional Truths

* Without Him, I can do nothing (John 15:5).
* The goodness of God leads to repentance (Romans 2:4).

To me, these truths are no longer just words on a page—they are the reality that shapes how I think, speak, and live.

Walking in my new identity doesn't mean life is without challenges, because, believe me, the challenges keep coming. But it does mean that I no longer let myself be defined by them. My worth can no longer be measured by my performance, but by the finished work of Jesus on the cross.

I was growing in my confidence that God's plans for me are good:

> *"For I know the thoughts that I think toward you, saith the Lord, thoughts of peace and not of evil, and to give you an expected end. Then shall ye call upon me, and ye shall go and pray unto me, and I will hearken unto you."*
> (Jeremiah 29:11-12 KJV)

I was standing on the promises of God, rooted in His truth. But God wasn't finished with me yet.

Living in my new identity did not erase the deep wounds of my past. Those hurts—some I had buried —still had a way of rising to the surface, shaping my reactions and weighing on my soul. My mind was learning the truth, but my heart still carried scars that needed healing.

It was time for God to do surgery—not on my circumstances but on the hidden places of my heart. I was about to learn that the health of my spiritual heart mattered just as much as the renewal of my mind.

Chapter 7
Spiritual Heart Health

"For out of the abundance of the heart his mouth speaks."
(Luke 6:45 NKJV)

I WAS BEGINNING TO understand that I was on a slow, divine journey. My past hurts were not going to go away with a few well-chosen verses. Accepting Jesus's forgiveness was only the beginning.

He gently walked me through divine encounters that changed my view and my behaviors. I found a cute paperback called *The Hurt,* by Teddi Doleski. This sweet story, told in my words, was an easy read, and I enjoyed reading it to my children. In this narrative.

Follow the journey of Justin, a joyful little boy, and his best friend, Gabriel:

> One day, Gabriel says something hurtful—just one unkind word—and

Justin is crushed. Instead of letting it go, Justin holds onto the hurt. He thinks about it often, feeding it with every memory of what Gabriel said.

At first, the hurt is small—just a quiet ache in his chest. But then it begins to grow. It takes over his bed, then spills into his closet. Soon, the hurt has taken over his entire room, leaving Justin feeling crowded, uncomfortable, and confused. The once-happy space he loved is now filled with something he never asked for.

Justin comes to a powerful realization: *If I don't let go of this hurt, it's going to push me out of my room.* With courage, Justin makes a brave choice —to forgive. And as he forgives, something incredible happens. The hurt begins to shrink. Little by little, it loses its power. Day by day, it disappears. Until one morning, it's gone. Completely. Like Justin, I had been very experienced in holding on to the pain of rejection. I had so many hurts from my childhood and teen years. It was a challenge to begin examining that pain. Holding onto hurt kept me bound to these painful experiences and hindered my ability to receive the goodness of God that I yearned to know and experience. I had made many attempts to renew my mind, and it was helping. But I was yet to be set free from the trauma of that season of my life.

The pattern of trying and failing has kept me from achieving my goals, but God reminded me of His grace, which is always sufficient. His grace changed me without the pressure to do it on my own.

I have a girlfriend who, amid a painful divorce, shared a powerful dream she believed was from the Lord. She saw a beautiful golden birdcage with the door wide open, yet the bird inside, representing herself—wouldn't fly out. Though the cage no longer held her, she had been confined for so long that she couldn't move past it. God was showing her that she had been set free but needed to embrace that freedom. The dream reminded her of the words "He came to set the captives free" from the Bible.

There is a familiar story about a man visiting a circus, and it goes like this:

> "As a man was passing the elephants, he suddenly stopped, confused by the fact that these huge creatures were being held by only a small rope tied to their front leg. No chains, no cages. It was obvious that the elephants could, at any time, break away from their bonds, but for some reason, they did not.
>
> He saw a trainer nearby and asked why these animals just stood there

and made no attempt to get away. 'Well,' the trainer said, 'when they are very young and much smaller, we use the same size rope to tie them, and at that age, it's enough to hold them. As they grow up, they are conditioned to believe they cannot break away. They believe the rope can still hold them, so they never try to break free.

The man was amazed. These animals **could** at any time break free from their bonds, but because they believed they couldn't, they were stuck right where they were.

Like the elephants, how many of us go through life hanging onto a belief that we cannot do something, simply because we failed at it once before?"[2]

I came to understand just how easy it is to live like a chained elephant—believing that because I couldn't do something before, I'd never be able to do it. I've been trapped by that lie more times than I care to admit.

Guarding Your Heart

Our heart is the very center of our being. We are spirit. We have a soul. We live in a body. Most of us carry some hurt in our hearts—wounds we haven't fully dealt with. Some of us are fighters—we push back against the pain with force. Others are stuffers—we bury the pain, hoping we'll never have to face it again. This causes us to guard our hearts by keeping them away from people and God. One thing is true: we were not created to carry unresolved pain forever.

When our hearts are stressed, our bodies respond. Stress, negative thoughts, and anger release harmful chemicals into the bloodstream. Over time, this can have a significant impact on our physical health.

"Guard your heart above all else, for it determines the course of your life."
(Proverbs 4:23 NLT)

Guarding our hearts in a positive way, as this Scripture talks about, is to protect us from evil.

I have a friend with an amazing story that illustrates how profoundly the issues of the heart can impact the body.

Years ago, she called and asked me to pray for her twenty-five-year-old daughter. She had been rushed to the ER with a dangerously rapid heart rate and was admitted to the hospital. Her condition was so severe that she couldn't get out of bed without assistance, not even to go to the bathroom. For four days, the doctors ran tests but found nothing physically wrong.

After ruling out every other possibility, the final diagnosis was broken heart syndrome—a condition brought on by extreme emotional stress.

According to medical sources, "People with broken heart syndrome may have sudden chest pain or think they're having a heart attack. Broken heart syndrome affects just part of the heart. It briefly interrupts the way the heart pumps blood. The rest of the heart continues to work as usual. Though rare, broken heart syndrome is powerful proof that our thoughts, stress, and emotional wounds can directly impact our physical bodies."[3]

My friend knew that her daughter hadn't fully healed from losing the love of her life. But now with a precise diagnosis, they both had answers. My friend's daughter came to a turning point when the understanding she received gave her the strength to let go of the past and begin a new chapter. It was the miracle her mother had been praying for.

But God wasn't done. The $10,000 hospital bill—something they had no way to pay—was forgiven entirely. The hospital applied a benevolence fund to the account, and she walked away owing nothing. That, too, was a miracle —our God is amazing!

The medical term for the heart is *cardia,* derived from the Greek word *kardia,* meaning "the core of your being." When we experience deep pain, regret, or heartbreak, our heart suffers. We replay our mistakes, drown in "what-ifs" and "if-onlys," and start believing the lies that say it's all our fault.

But we have a choice.

We don't have to let rejection, loss, or heartbreak control us. We don't have to listen to the lies of the enemy.

Once I began to understand this revelation, I decided—no more! No more torment. No more shame. From now on, I reject every lie that tries to take root in my mind and heart. I choose truth. I choose freedom. I choose to guard my heart, the core of who I am, and ask God for the grace to walk forward in peace.

Meditative Scripture to Transform Your Mind

- "Create in me a clean heart, O God, and renew a right spirit within me" (Psalm. 51:10 KJV).
- "All things work together for good to them that love God" (Romans 8:28 KJV).
- We are blessed with all spiritual blessings (Ephesians1:3, paraphrased).

I used to think healing was a moment. Now I know— it's a process. It's a slow unraveling of the lies I believed about myself, stitched back together with truth and love by God's grace.

Protecting my heart didn't mean building walls. It meant giving God full access to every room or space in my heart—the broken, the buried, the bolted shut —all of it exposed to Him so that He could heal. It also meant laying down control and self-protecting measures. To heal, I must trust in my Healer.

Whether it's the quiet ache of rejection, the trauma of profound loss, or the weight of years that have gone badly, God doesn't ask us to fix it. He asks us to bring it to His feet and trust Him to do what only He can—restore our hearts, renew our minds, and lead us into freedom.

Our heart matters to God. Every part of us matters to Him. We must never forget—we matter to the One who created us.

Today, I choose to believe that I am free and that what God began in me, He will accomplish to its finish. It helps me to meditate on this. Join with me:

The time is now. It's never too late.
We are redeemable. We are never too far gone.
He will finish His good work in us.
This is our time to fly.

Chapter 8

Understanding Kingdom Authority

"... in the kingdom of light ..."
(Colossians 1:12 NIV)

ONLY THREE MONTHS had passed since I surrendered my life and made Jesus Lord over everything. I was living in unfamiliar spiritual territory—stepping into the wonder of the unseen and discovering peace in His presence. Any chance I got, I'd slip away to be alone with God. I craved those quiet places, those sacred encounters that settled my heart.

Then came a special day—a day of divine connection.

I found that Elly, who had become both a dear friend and spiritual mentor (and the only one who could truly help with Alison's unique needs), was also Rose's best friend, my closest SEAL wife companion.

That morning, Rose and I headed to Elly's waterfront home for the first time. It was a mid-July day in Virginia Beach—sunny and clear. The weather seemed to mirror the warmth we felt as we pulled into the driveway.

I was in awe of Elly's gorgeous, elegant, and inviting home. The sunlight glistened across the water behind her house, making everything shimmer. On the patio sat a beautifully set table draped with a bright, cheerful tablecloth. Elly had adorned each place setting with three layers of plates, seashell napkin rings, gold-rimmed goblets, and a stunning fresh-flower centerpiece. It looked like something out of a magazine. I felt like a princess, honored to be invited to this lovely home for such a beautiful luncheon.

Suddenly, my mother's voice echoed in my heart: "Patti, mind your p's and q's, and be careful what you touch." Social settings like this always made me a little nervous, and I had expected a smaller gathering.

But as Elly's guests began to arrive, my nerves quickly faded. The women were warm, inviting, friendly, and stylish. I was glad we had arrived early so we could greet them one by one. I learned their names easily. A sense of welcome settled in my heart.

I had never experienced being in the company with such lovely women before, and I found myself wondering how Elly had gathered such a beautiful circle around her.

Of the six women I did not know, some were homemakers, while others were professionals. They came from different churches and walks of life. But one thing united us all, our deep love for Jesus.

As we sat at the table, Rose was to my left and Debbie to my right. Debbie was a slender woman with dark brown hair, light makeup, and a deep violet ensemble, complemented by a matching, flowing print scarf that gently swayed in the breeze. She was pleasant to talk with.

Elly called us together, and a hush fell over us as her prayer over the food began. It was thoughtful and flowed gracefully from her lips. I found her prayer moving and longed to pray in that way. I knew God was moving in me to learn to pray with the same kind of passion and fervor.

Before us on the table was a fruit salad with yogurt, featuring a hint of nutmeg and cinnamon. I knew this meal was going to be a treat. And indeed, it was. Elly's entrée was a recipe she learned while living in Belgium, just as decadent. The dessert was equally so. As elegant and delicious as the meal was, it did not compare to the rich conversation taking place around me at that table.

Debbie began to share a vision she had seen in prayer—a glimpse of the celestial kingdom, the New Jerusalem (see Rev. 21). She described ornate streets of gold and crystal walls, which emanated multiple colors. I could see it in my mind's eye as she spoke. I felt the presence of peace as she sat next to me. My heart stirred with longing.

I wanted to be in that kingdom, I mused. *I wanted what those women had.*

These women astounded me with their profound spiritual insights and deep love for their Lord and Savior. Their beauty went far beyond appearances. There was a radiant glow from deep within, and there was confidence and spiritual authority in them. I wanted that.

As the conversation flowed, the topics shifted to challenges in marriage, parenting, and relationships with parents and friends. They shared about how they prayed the Scriptures, how they clung to promises during storms, and how peace came through God's Word.

They were powerful women of wisdom who walked in authority and grace.

Wow, my mind was overwhelmed trying to grasp all that I had just experienced. And the wisdom and depth of these women were evident.

My mind spun, trying to take it all in. I was overwhelmed, in the best way possible, by the presence of God and the love of Jesus Christ radiating throughout the afternoon. I felt like royalty, sitting at that table with those beautiful women.

I have seen breathtaking sunrises and sunsets from Paris, France, and other cities around the world, but this was truly exceptional. I was captivated by the spiritual world that these women demonstrated during our prayer time together. It was otherworldly.

I left Elly's home that day with a new hunger. I wanted to learn. I wanted to grow. I wanted to walk in the same kind of presence and power. I became what I jokingly called a "spiritual junkie." I craved more of God, more of His Word, and more of the Kingdom. I silently prayed as I left, *"Lord, establish Your kingdom within me."*

I began studying every Scripture I could find about the Kingdom of God. I was stunned to learn that the Kingdom was not just a faraway place in heaven. It was within me. Learning how to access that truth was a journey that was only just beginning.

Rose saw I needed more support, so she introduced me to her friend Kathy for prayer and encouragement.

"She's a beautiful prayer warrior," Rose said.

"A what?" I blurted out. "What is a prayer warrior?"

"A prayer warrior is someone who chooses to pray for the needs of others using spiritual principles," she explained.

Oh YES! I thought. *That is exactly who I want in my inner circle.*

When we arrived at Kathy's, she opened the door before we could knock. Her thick brown hair bounced as she welcomed us with a radiant smile.

She knelt to greet my children, making them feel at ease and safe. I loved that she included them in the moment. We needed every bit of support we could get.

What happened next changed me.

Two hours flew by as I sat with these two women who knew how to pray, I mean...really pray like I had never heard before. Their words carried weight. Their connection to God's presence was tangible. As they prayed, I felt something lift off me. I didn't want to leave the joy in that room.

Kathy's prayer for Alison, specifically for her speech and motor skills, touched me. It gave me confidence that God saw us, and healing was on the way.

Before I left, Kathy handed me a grocery bag filled with books she had packed just for me. I walked out of her house with a full heart and new fire in my spirit. I had found a prayer partner—and a guide who would help me learn more of God's ways.

For the first time since leaving my career—the place where I was "somebody" known and respected—I realized God had something far greater for me. His plans were unfolding before my eyes.

The Authority of the Believer

Back at home, I emptied the grocery bag of books and laid them out on my bed. I held each one in my hands, asking God which to read first.

Then I saw it: a sword with light behind it—*The Authority of the Believer* by Kenneth Hagin. I knew instantly ... this is the one.

I devoured the book. It was as if someone had opened a door that had always been there, but I had never seen. It brought such refreshing.

One story in particular hit me hard. Hagin wrote about hiding a $20 bill in a secret compartment of his wallet and forgetting it was there. He had what he needed all along, but because he didn't remember it, he couldn't use it to get the gas he needed and remained stuck. That was me.

We must know what we have— and then we must use it.

While that book taught me about binding and loosing, I also learned that standing in spiritual authority and partnering with God was within my power according to the Bible. And God's power is already at work inside me.

"Now to Him who is able to do exceedingly abundantly above all that we ask or think, according to the power that works inside of us."
(Ephesians 3:20 KJV)

I realized this wasn't about me striving to have power—it was about His power given to me. All I had to do was believe and receive. And that shook me.

Nothing is too hard for You, God—not even me. I finally recognized—it's His power, not mine. I wasn't changing my life; He was. I asked God to move on my behalf and do what only He can do. And He did.

Nothing—absolutely nothing—is impossible for HIM!

The beauty of this declaration is that it includes ME. I had been sinking, stuck in fear and striving. But now? I stand on solid ground. He gave me the authority to step into the abundance He planned for me all along. I just needed to claim what was already mine—like going to a store and picking something off the shelf, except Jesus already paid for it. My heavenly account is marked "Paid in Full" because of what my Abba Father has done.

WOW, WHAT A CONCEPT! I had a hard time wrapping my head around all the blessings He has for me.

In the Kingdom, it is mine by divine order, because it was always part of His plan to bless me.

The truth shook me. This truth was not hellfire and brimstone or condemnation. It was a loving God who longs to pour out good things.

But the questions echoed in my heart: *Do I believe it? Do I receive it? Do I really trust that these blessings are for me?*

I laid the Bible on my chest and wrestled with the weight of what I had just read and the gravity of those questions.

He is not a respecter of persons. What He's done for others, He will do for me. That is His nature. That is His will. From the foundation of the earth, He designed a life of abundance and blessing for His children, and I am one of them. Now it is up to me to believe it, receive it, and walk in it!

Spiritual Laws at Work

Did you know spiritual laws are operating in your life, whether you're aware of them or not? I didn't.

But as I look back, I realize I was unknowingly tapping into spiritual principles long before I understood them or could explain them. I refused to believe the negative words spoken over me. Deep down, I knew I was created for more. I kept hoping, and I chose to stay positive. I focused my thoughts on what I wanted, not what I feared. And somehow ... things began to shift.

Why? Because spiritual laws work—even if we don't know they're at work.

Similar to physical laws, the Law of Gravity is true even if you don't understand it. Understanding gravity is not necessary to keep you grounded. You don't need a degree in Law of Aerodynamics to board an airplane—you get on, trusting it will take you where you want to go.

The same is true with spiritual laws. God, in His goodness, laid them out in Scripture—not to confuse or burden us, but to bless us. These laws are consistent, trustworthy, and for our benefit. They govern how the Kingdom operates. And when we align with them, we unlock heaven's flow in our everyday lives. Like in the Law of Sowing and Reaping from Proverbs 3:9-10, a major key that helped change my spiritual life.

For me, I learned that I must give or sow into the good things that I would like to reap. I can do this with my words, too.

There are things in my heart that I long to do or become—desires I had not ever dared to speak out loud before.

God put those desires in me. In us. He's a big God! HE WILL DO EXCEEDINGLY MORE because of His power that works on the inside of us!

Why does He do this?

Because He Can. And—more importantly—because **He wants to.**

Life with God is overflowing with blessings. But the question remains: **Do we believe that?**

SEE IT, SAY IT, BELIEVE IT, RECEIVE IT!

That's not just a catchy formula from motivational speakers—it's biblically based and the framework for activating faith.

Tony Horton, known for transforming bodies through his fitness programs, used these same principles. As an overweight man chasing a goal, he visualized what he wanted, wrote it down, spoke it out, and believed it would come to pass. That's how he saw the change he wanted.

Again, that's how spiritual laws work. They work for Tony Horton and are available to anyone who applies them.

Because they are not just motivational— they are spiritual.

SEE IT:

God told a 75-year-old, childless Abraham: "I will make you into a great nation, and I will bless you" (Genesis 12:2 NKJV). Years later, still without a child, God took him outside and said:

*"Look up at the sky and count the stars...so
shall your offspring be."*
(Genesis 15:5 NIV)

God gave him a vision so vivid that it
overwhelmed his present reality. Why? Because
what we see shapes what we believe.

SAY IT:

*"Call those things which be not as
though they were."*
(Romans 4:17 KJV)

Speak it. Declare it. Speak life, not lack. Speak
what God says, not what fear says. Our words
have power when they align with God's Word. He
has the best gifts for His children.

BELIEVE IT:

*"And Abraham believed the Lord and He
(God) accounted it to him for
righteousness."*
(Genesis 15:6 KJV)

Abraham had every reason to doubt. And yes, he faltered. He tried to fulfill God's promise in his own way. But God reminded him:

> *"This one [Speaking of Ishmael] shall not be your heir, but one who will come from your own body shall be your heir."*
> **(Genesis 5:4 NKJV)**

Faith means trusting even when you don't see.

> *"Faith is the substance of things hoped for, the evidence of things not seen."*
> **(Hebrews 11:1 KJV)**

It's in the waiting where we're most tempted to waver. But it is also in the waiting that our faith is forged in the fire.

RECEIVE IT:

> *"What things soever ye desire, when ye pray, believe that ye receive them, and ye shall have them."*
> **(Mark 11:24 KJV)**

At 100 years old—25 years after the promise was made—Abraham finally held Isaac, his promised son.

Whew, that is a long time to hold on to a promise. But God's Word never fails. He's not slow; He's precise.

So, I ask you:

What do you want?

What has God whispered to your heart that you have been afraid to write down, let alone speak aloud?

Write it down, Speak it. Believe it. Receive It.

"Write the vision and make it plain on tablets, That he may run who reads it" (Habakkuk 2:2 NKJV). Because if God said it, it will come to pass. And when it does, you'll know.

Spiritual laws work.

Scripture to Transform Your Mind

- "Now unto him that is able to do exceedingly abundantly above all that we ask or think, according to the power that worketh in us" (Ephesians 3:20 KJV).

- "God, who gives life to the dead and calls those things which do not exist as though they did" (Romans 4:17 NKJV).

- "… even God, who quickeneth the dead, and calleth those things which be not as though they were" (Romans 4:17 KJV).

Our God is great, and he can and wants to give you good things. Do you believe that?

"...for out of the abundance of the heart, the mouth speaks."
(Matthew 12:34 NKJV)

Chapter 9
Increased Faith

"For assuredly, I say unto you, whoever says to this mountain, 'Be removed and cast into the sea,' and does not doubt in his heart, but believes that what he says will be done, he will have whatever he says."
(Mark 11:23 NKJV)

One Bucketload at a Time

ONE DAY, I WAS driving across a bridge over the lake near my home. I spotted a bulldozer and a dump truck slowly chipping away at the mountainside. Each day as I passed, I watched the progress—one bucket at a time, one truckload at a time. It was slow, and sometimes seemingly tedious, but they were relentless. With time, a valuable, empty, flat lot lay at this lakeside plot. Eventually, that rugged mountain became the perfect home for the ENGLISH MUFFIN, a charming lakeside café. What a joy it was to sip coffee on the sunny patio, watching the water sparkle—and every time I was reminded: **persistent faith moves mountains.**

I took a spiritual perspective on this visual lesson and realized that a mountain was anything that stood in the way of attaining the results I felt needed to be transformed. There were three things I saw as mountains in my life that I wanted to change:

1. Negative thinking
2. Getting short with my children
3. Financial Lack

Mountain of Negative Thinking: Many buckets were used to remove the hindrances of soul-crushing thoughts that would come through my mind. I call those evil thoughts "negative talk," and that leads to negative confession, which in turn leads to negative actions. Out of the abundance of the heart, the mouth speaks. Now, I have made a conscious effort to observe the thoughts in my mind. I would disagree with those thoughts and replace them with positive ones.

Mountain of Short Temper: I felt inadequate to parent my children. I wondered if they were suffering without having their father around more frequently, and whether I was enough. Was it my fault that Alison had delayed speech and was unable to complete a task? Did I fail her in some way that had held her back? Could I have done more? My inadequacies caused anger and frustration to rise quickly. Those unhealthy feelings had to go. I declared the truth of God's word like a mantra. Repeatedly, I would say to myself, "I was and am more than enough." He chose me to parent these precious gifts, and He would be faithful to help me do what He has called me to.

Mountain of Financial Lack: There was warfare in my mind, especially when money was short. I could work, but I believed God told me to stay at home with my children. To help with finances, I would watch the little ones for the mothers instead of participating in the weekly Bible study. In that decision came His provision. I would get twenty dollars. Then I went straight to the grocery store and purchased milk, bread, peanut butter, and some fruit. God provided every time.

This analogy taught me to see each step as a forward motion—one step or bucket at a time.

It took time to clear the land of all three mountains in my life, but I persisted in seeing, writing, and declaring the truth. And in time, I did see the fruits of my labor. I released my faith to move my mountain and see the change that I desired.

Speak the Word

Music is powerful. Your body starts toe-tapping and head-bobbing to the rhythm. Singers wield emotions, creating tears with a single note. And those glass-shattering pitches? That's just physics —high-frequency vibrations hitting the right resonance. Booming bass? It's low-end waves shaking the world, knocking stuff from shelves.

Mozart, a deaf composer, felt the music's pulse through the ground and vibrations speaking what his ears couldn't hear. Music's not just sound—it's a physical force, reaching into your soul and surroundings. The spoken word is like music in that it creates vibrations through the sound of your voice.

We either create or destroy with our words. Is that why God's word says:

> **"Death and Life are in the power of the tongue."**
> **(Proverbs 18:21 NKJV)**

I once read a book, *Quantum Faith,* that says:

"Faith is an unseen energy force. It is not matter, but it creates matter and actually becomes matter. The faith that you use to call forth the manifestation of healing or finances changes form when the manifestation takes place. That is because faith-energized words convert energy to matter. Words are the catalyst to turn the substance of faith into a physical manifestation. Faith is the raw material from which all matter is made. Hebrews 11:1 says that "faith is the substance ...." It is the invisible substance from which your physical world was and is created."[4]

Faith energized words: speak life to your future.

Jesus said, "The words that I speak unto you, they are spirit, and they are life" (John 6:63 KJV).

Each Saturday, Doug and I looked forward to boating during sunset, where the water sparkled in the changing light. The lake water was turbulent due to the numerous boats competing for space. The turbulent water was an accurate picture of our demeanor. We left home fighting about no particular thing—just angry at one another.

Once we were in the boat, I said something that clearly rubbed Doug the wrong way, although I don't remember what it was. His anger increased, and he responded by slamming the accelerator to full throttle, causing the boat to go airborne on the wake. I was in the front of the boat. It was as if things were in slow motion. My knee hit the deck, and my foot was caught on the seat. The pain was immediate, and the tears streamed as I cried out in pain.

Doug immediately turned the boat around, but hit every wake, sending excruciating pain in my leg that felt like it was shooting out of my brain.

I tried to put on a brave face, but it was the worst pain of my life, and that included childbirth.

Doug's anger was now replaced with sympathy, or was it regret, I wondered? Whatever the case, his demeanor became more of a protector, and the anger was gone. Docking the boat, he gently lifted me out and carried me to the car.

We drove twenty-five minutes to the emergency room. By the time we arrived, "I'm sorry," had been said by both of us.

An MRI (a test that shows muscles and ligaments) confirmed that I had a torn ACL, the ligament inside my knee joint. I was entirely denying what had happened. However, the pain that was not relieved with their medication was mocking me.

Facing the proposed one-year process of surgery, recovery, and rehabilitation was depressing. It had occurred to me that our scheduled vacation, just a few days away, was ruined. I could not go on crutches. I was filled with sadness, and maybe even a little anger.

But then it hit me ... *Patti, are you going to whine about what happened, or are you going to do what you've been studying?*

I changed my mind and began praising the Lord and declaring the truth of His Word. I remembered what Annette Capp said, "Praise creates."

I began professing words of praise and truth, and the day came for us to leave on vacation. I was determined to "not grow weary while doing good, for in due season we shall reap if we do not lose heart" (Galatians 6:9 NKJV).

I learned to release my faith through my words as I recited Scriptures; my words shifted things into what God had already planned for me. Not allowing the pain I was feeling to determine what came out of my mouth, I began to agree with His will and plan for my life. I AM HEALED.

On the twenty-one-hour drive, I praised the Lord that I could walk. The tears streamed down my face the entire car ride due to pain. I was completely miserable, and the reality was that I was still on crutches. But I kept saying "I am healed. I know God is my healer" as a mantra of my conviction.

The week of vacation was an exercise in smiling through the pain and in letting my family have a good time for the Fourth of July.

When we finally got home, I used a small, wheeled desk chair to get around and continued to praise the Lord for being able to walk and play tennis. I declared out loud, "I am healed, and I can walk and run."

The surgical appointment was still weeks out, and Doug was faithful to pack up the kids and take us to church on Sundays.

One particular Sunday, the preacher stopped mid-sermon and looked straight at me. He said, "Do you want to be healed?"

"Yes," I answered.

"Come up here."

I reached for my crutches.

"No," he said firmly. "Come without them."

I looked at the pastor's wife and thought, *WHAT? HOW?* A little panicked with a frown of disagreement on my face, I wondered just how I was going to get up there! I stood up on one leg, thinking for those few seconds, *Now, how am I going to get up there?*

I reached out to my husband sitting next to me. His heart was still tender towards me because of what happened. I had forgiven him and myself for our anger more than once because forgiveness is a process. With Doug on one side and my pastor's wife on the other, I got up and hobbled up to the altar for prayer.

The pastor told me, "Go back and forth from here to the door three times."

I looked at him like he had three heads, "WHAT?" I knew this was a faith walk. I hobbled, with the support of my husband and Maryann, the pastor's wife, down the center aisle to touch the door. With each step, I could apply slightly more pressure to the stance as I progressed forward. By the third trip, I noticed the pain easing. Each step was a step toward healing. By the time I got outside, the pain was gone. I WAS HEALED! WOW! God always moved on my behalf and still does.

I must admit, my faith grew by leaps and bounds in that moment. My heart was so full of God's love. And I was living in what the Bible says in Isaiah:

"God's word will not return void but will accomplish the thing for which it is sent."

SO, THIS WAS IT! This is what Annette Capps was speaking about—a creative force of faith to bring healing to my body. I personally experienced a creative miracle.

Knowing the truth was now supported by experiencing His truth. I was so excited that I wanted to tell everyone that they, too, could be healed.

Here are my key takeaways after this experience:

- Speak my mountain into motion: keep it moving even if it looks like a shovel vs a bucket.
- Speak life when it looks hopeless: don't give up on doing the good thing.
- Speak a breakthrough even when in crisis: I can't doubt. I have to believe it is coming.
- Speak health over suffering: this was particularly challenging, but I had to remind myself that my words have power.
- Speak God's Word, His promise over impossibility. Remember Isaiah 55:11 (NIV):

"So is my word that goes out from my mouth: It will not return to me empty but will accomplish what I desire and achieve the purpose for which I sent it."

The following is an example of how I prayed for myself. Feel free to use it if you are struggling:

I speak to my spirit, and I declare:

Be strengthened in the power of God's Word. Do not despair or give up.

Even in the darkness, life is not lost—hope is not lost. The Kingdom of God is alive and active within you. Lift your eyes and see the fullness of the Kingdom of God operating within your life.

Let the glory of Jesus shine upon you now. Let His light break through the darkness of your world, breaking any heavy place. His light shines in the darkness, and the darkness cannot comprehend it.

Lord, I pray—deliver me from the things I struggle with. The things I can't fix. The things that weigh heavily on my heart. Break off the situations that don't align with Your Word and aren't part of Your Kingdom.

Open my spiritual eyes. Let me see, really see! To behold and understand who You are and the fullness of Your provision for me right now.

In the powerful name of Jesus,

Amen.

A couple more Scriptures to bring encouragement:

- "Behold, I will pour out my Spirit unto you, I will make known my words unto you" (Proverbs 1:23 KJV).

- "Beloved, I pray that you may prosper in all things and be in health, just as your soul prospers" (3 John 1:2 NKJV).

Chapter 10
When Obedience Leads to Provision

*"If you are willing and obedient, you shall eat
the good of the land."*
(Isaiah 1:19 NKJV)

THERE ARE SIXTY-FIVE Scriptures on obeying the Word of God. That alone should tell us something: obedience matters. It's the key that unlocks faith in action. We have to believe—not just that He is —but that He is the rewarder of those who diligently seek Him.

For me, submissive obedience wasn't just a spiritual concept; it became the lifeline to provision, peace, and all the promises of God. Especially in the chaos of military life, when married to a Navy SEAL. Every day was a question mark. Would he be called today? Would he come home soon—or at all? I didn't want to leave the house, just in case I missed his call.

Six years later, it was still not easy. Three months into my salvation, I began learning to place my hope in God, not the Navy schedule. I had found a new trust, a new light, a hope that everything was going to be alright.

Doug was gone for the whole summer on a Temporary Duty (TDY) training in Indiana. That summer felt simple. Mornings were quiet—I spent time reading the Bible, encouraging books, and reflecting on who God was and how to respond to Him. This time filled my heart with so much peace; it was more precious to me than gold. I loved to linger and bask in His presence.

Our sunshine-filled days had an easy rhythm: breakfast, swimsuits, and the military pool or the beach. When I reached the water's edge, I found a release from the pressures that weighed heavily on my mind, like walking around with a ton of bricks. My sun-kissed babies, aglow, were jumping at the bit to get into the water.

Here at this place of fun, four-year-old Alison was learning to swim like a pro. Brandon, all of eighteen months, splashed happily in the crook of my arm. Every so often, I realized—Oops—I forgot to keep his face above water. But he was a quick learner and soon figured out how to lift his head and stay afloat. By summer's end, both kids could swim. Alison jumped off the diving board with ease, swimming as hard as she could to get to the ladder. All the while, she was laughing. She was so happy with herself that she climbed up the ladder and trotted back in line to go again. Brandon, waiting for his turn, climbed on the diving board.

The lifeguard saw him and shouted, "Get that kid off the board!"

I waved at the lifeguard, beaming from ear to ear, "He knows how to swim."

About that time, Brandon jumped, swam to the ladder, climbed out like it was nothing, and then lined up to go again. Laughing the whole way.

I was so proud because I felt like I was mastering this single-parenting thing. I wanted my love for the water, whether it was the beach or the pool, to inspire my children's passion for it too. The three of us had built something beautiful together. Teaching them to swim was vital. I knew we would always be around water, so I needed to ensure they were proficient in understanding water safety. One would think that Doug would be the one to teach them to swim. After all, he was an Iowa state swimming champion. I just knew Doug would be elated to see his water babies thriving, and I am the proud Mama who taught them.

Longing for Doug to be home, I missed the warmth of his embrace, and I had time to reflect on my ways. I wanted to be a better wife. I read all the verses about wives being submissive to their husbands. I thought *this wouldn't be too hard. I can do this.* On our phone calls, I made sure not to be combative or pushy. I was proud of myself—obedient and supportive. As for submission to my husband? *I've got this and will nail it!* Or so I thought.

Doug was due to return from his temporary duty station, where he was training to become a hospital corpsman. It was hurricane season, and Hurricane Gloria was headed straight for North Carolina and Virginia Beach, and we lived five miles from the ocean. I was prepared—flashlights, food, coolers, candles.

Alone and with the two little ones to care for, I brushed aside all negative thoughts of "what if" this or that happened. This was not my first major hurricane, but it looked like it would pack a punch on Virginia Beach, near the center of landfall. I felt capable and confident.

Then the phone rang.

As always, I rushed to answer it, hoping it was Doug, and it was. All the wonderful pleasantries were exchanged—logistics of when he was leaving, and so on. But there was more that Doug wanted to say. Breaking the information softly and gently, he said, "Honey, I want to move to California."

His words hit me as hard as any hurricane could.

No, no, no, not again, the thought screaming in my head.

After a long silence, I said, "California is so far away." Making sure my tone was pleasant. I was waiting for him to change his mind. But his deep breaths told me that was not going to happen. Tension grew within me; I just knew in my heart he was not going to move from this idea.

Why, oh why can't we just stay here?

I have a life, and it is beautiful, ignoring the fact that he was not here. Frustration grew inside of me. This battle with my thoughts was raging back and forth like a washing machine that would not quit.

Three years earlier, we had this discussion. The military had even shipped our furniture to California, and I refused to go. I had been stubborn and told Doug I was NOT moving to

California. He went in and told his detailer that his wife is not moving, and to ship our household effects back. Doug had gone to bat for me on that one. This time, however, I heard in his voice and attitude that there was a determination that this scenario would not change.

Now here we were again.

I felt confused and stunned at first. Everything in me wanted to let Doug have it with both barrels. But I stayed silent, even with the raging, disbelieving thoughts at war within me.

Why can't we just stay here?

I loved my life. I had friends and a church family. Stability. My kids were thriving. I was finally growing in God's Word. But I remembered: obedience precedes blessing. I couldn't see it, I didn't understand it, but I knew I had to be obedient because this was Doug's desire. I would have to trust God.

So, I took a deep breath, pressed my lips together, exhaled, and said, "Okay." My heart would eventually catch up to my words.

Doug didn't rejoice, say thank you, or in any way indicate that he was excited with my response, even though he was fully aware that I didn't want to leave Virginia Beach. He just said, "I'm driving home after a few hours of rest." And then confirmed, "I have the orders to California in my hands."

I reminded him of Hurricane Gloria. "Please don't push it, Honey. I'm not sure it's safe to drive right now."

Doug responded the way you might expect the invincible Navy SEAL to answer, "If I drive now, I will be ok driving through it."

I don't know why I was surprised. This guy of mine had a habit of taking chances, and I could not sway his decision. Honestly, I was excited to see him in just fourteen hours.

Listening to the weather all night long made me grateful that I had developed a strong prayer life. The winds whipped the palm trees with a violence like that of a rag doll. As the storm raged outside, I relied on prayer through the night: "Lord, bring him home safely, put your angels around him and the truck. Keep him awake and aware. Give him strength and give me peace."

The night seemed endless, with the wind howling and things hitting the windows, accompanied by distant sounds of bangs and booms. I made a conscious effort to keep peace in my mind and prayed as I went in and out of sleep, during the long, lingering night.

When the morning light finally shone in the sky, debris was everywhere: palm branches, shingles, siding, floating down the street that now looked more like a river. I couldn't leave the house because the water had risen to the door. Only boats were paddled along the streets now. Praise the Lord, the hurricane did not hit us. Thank you, Jesus, for answering my prayers!

I wondered how Doug was. As I write this now, I find myself considering how having a cell phone might have changed my anxious heart. A quick check-in and then all would seem well with the world. But instead, I prayed with only the knowledge in my heart that all would be well and continued to pray for his safe return.

Hours seemed like days. Sitting, waiting on pins and needles, and wondering how Doug was doing. I checked the phone a few times to see if we still had phone service. We did.

I understood *that* he had to wait until he found a pay phone to call me, or when he stopped to get gas. I reassured myself, *he'd call soon. He probably didn't want to wake me.*

I sat reflecting on what my life looked like now that I was married to a Navy SEAL, processing the information about moving again. Four moves in six years—I have left friends and community, and I hardly knew the meaning of stability. But as a woman, fully trained in the life of being a SEAL Team wife, I made a mental list of the things that needed to be done.

I appreciated the opportunities Doug had to advance his career. I had grown accustomed to following in his footsteps, and admittedly, I had fantastic experiences, such as camping in Europe for three weeks with our fully packed car—a very unusual sight in Europe—and vacationing in the town of Gibraltar, where I climbed the Rock of Gibraltar in the Mediterranean Sea. I have seen so many things that have shaped me positively. This move would be a new and interesting place for me as well, so I encouraged myself to look on the positive side.

I tried to remind myself where else he could go. There were only a few detachments where SEAL teams could go around the world, and we had already filled one of them when we lived in England, when we were first married, which meant he could not fill it again. Only those with glowing recommendations got that SEAL appointment. That left the East Coast and West Coast teams. The Seal Community was not that large. *Why is he feeling the need for a change? What am I missing? What makes that man unable to settle?* I wondered.

I didn't want to let go of the comfortable life I had here in Virginia Beach, including my friends, my church, and my kids' routines. My mentors and my church had been faithful to help me grow in my Christian walk. I struggled; I did not want to make this move. It would dramatically change my life.

The ache in my heart was immense. I knew the pattern. I would be taken to California and dropped off, despite his reassurance that he would be there. "We would be together, as a family," he said. If only this were true.

Starting over and trying to find friends, a church, and a support group, my mind grappled with the weight of the unknown. *What about Alison? How will this affect her?* I learned she needs consistency. I now find myself in unwelcome territory—no, I am in worry mode. *Think positive! Think positive*, I reminded myself.

Suddenly, I heard Doug at the door. Whew—all my worries faded. He walked in, wrapped me in his big, strong arms, which filled me with hope that everything would be alright. He kissed and hugged the kids and me, said a few kind words, sorted out a few things, and then turned his attention to the task at hand. MOVING.

I wanted to know how he made it through the flooded streets, but there was no time for that. He was a man of action.

He called the Joint Personal Property Shipping Office (JPPSO). The person said, "Come in now if you can make it."

I thought, *surely, he would not go back out in this disaster zone.*

Again, why did I still have the ability to be surprised by his bravery … or insanity … depending on who you ask.

Doug, Brandon, Alison, and I piled hurriedly into the truck and were on our way less than an hour later. I would soon find out how he made it

111

through the flooded streets. It turned out that a truck was so much better than my car.

With great care, he navigated the streets of the hurricane aftermath. The streets were lined with massive, mature trees that were knocked over like bowling pins.

Since we were the only people on the road, we arrived at our destination in half the time it would have taken us. We walked in and took a seat. The paperwork was ready to go in an hour, and we walked out with dates for the pickup of our belongings. All this for a TDY assignment of only six months, but he would be home for the assignment, and I was counting my blessings that we would be together.

We had to prepare three shipments in six days: the express shipment contained only essential belongings needed to settle in our new home. We were limited to 500 pounds. Another shipment would be stored here in Virginia Beach. The rest of our belongings would be packed into a moving van and shipped to California.

Driving home was a mental aerobics workout that every military family learns—the methodical checklist that you execute upon immediate arrival home. The two little ones running around would add extra fun to the workout.

We walked in, and a flurry of activity commenced—three piles for three shipments.

No downtime. No relaxation. I was a bit frustrated because I had planned to share with him the work that God had done in me. But that was all shoved to the back burner—like so many things, when all your communication is in brief phone calls.

It was all hands-on deck. I wanted to take time to enjoy Doug being home, but there was much to do. I curiously asked myself, *Why the rush to get out of here? Why did he add stress to our lives and make our moving process so short?* I could feel the mental gymnastics calming as I released my turmoil to the Holy Spirit in prayer. I had a feeling that everything was going to be okay.

Six days passed quickly, and I was ready. I had a list of all the items that would go into each truck. Organization was key to getting us to our new location and reducing the likelihood of anger flaring.

The movers showed up, and by the end of the day, my life had been thrown into the back of a moving van. All that was left were the things we would take in our truck. I waved goodbye to our first home we purchased.

Westward we go ... At 5 pm, with our truck packed and the BMW on a trailer. A fifty-hour drive across country, and we would start all over again, building our lives in a new state. Ready or not, California, here we come.

Five days of driving allowed for much time to reminisce. *I didn't even get to say goodbye to my friends and church family. Who was I going to miss? Did I leave anything undone? Will the realtor get a renter for our home? I wish I were*

brave enough to help drive a truck pulling a trailer.
But I wasn't.

Though I longed to talk with Doug, it didn't seem like the right time, so we focused on the details of the move and entertaining Alison, now five years old, and Brandon, two and a half. That, in itself, was a full-time job. We played games and sang songs. Anything to help keep the kids busy, which was not an easy task in the days before iPads and car movies.

There was a moment of joy and laughter brought about by Brandon's two-foot "My Buddy," who was just so cute with his blue ball cap and freckles. We put him in the driver's seat of the BMW, and he looked so real. We loved to watch people take double-takes as they passed by. Many would laugh and wave. We laughed and waved back.

As expected, the sudden move was met with financial struggles, including moving expenses, restaurant meals, hotel rooms, and gas; we felt the pinch. Military lodging is very affordable and helpful, but it was already booked.

By day five, we set up our campsite. Not surprisingly for a Navy SEAL family, we traveled with all of our camping gear. Our motto was, "Never leave home without it."

Our half-dome, four-person tent was easy and fun for the kids to crawl in and out of. They were used to it. Instead of a clean hotel room and private shower, I got the joy of a communal campground shower, where I somehow felt dirtier after bathing than before. I washed the kids, though I'm not sure you could tell. The moment we stepped out, the dirt was back, clinging to everything; the tent, the chairs, probably even our toothbrushes, though I didn't check.

I mean, why did I bother cleaning anything when we were surrounded by the San Diego desert dirt, scrubby plants that barely cleared our ankles? The night was a bit rough as well. Sleeping on rock-laden ground with only a military-grade ground pad, which was not very cushioned, resulted in an irritable night's sleep for me. Admittedly, this woman was stretched!

Traditionally, I have enjoyed camping, especially the simple pleasure of cooking pancakes on the griddle. I simply added water to the container, shook, and poured. Voila! The smell of those pancakes over the campfire was irresistible. Of course, I enjoyed these delicious pancakes with sugary sweet syrup. It gave me a bit of extra energy, which was much needed after the rocky night. But the extra energy it gave my children … I did NOT need. That was not a brilliant move.

Breakfast done, gear stowed, children in the car, and we were ready to drive to our new home.

Driving over the Coronado Bridge was breathtaking. I had been to many places around the world, but oh my, this was beautiful. The sun was glistening on the water. You could see the bay and the ocean at the same time as you reached the top of the bridge. The bridge was tall enough to allow the aircraft carriers to pass underneath.

The military ships, yachts, and sailboats dotted the water.

As we crossed the bridge, Doug explained our choices for our six-month home. He had received his training in the area and was well-versed in it.

In our price range, there were two choices—slim pickings!

1. An itsy-bitsy house, called an Alley House because you walked past the large front of the house, down the sidewalk to reach the back, and/or entered through the Alley. The house was clean and freshly painted. The bonus for Doug was that it was close to work and would save an hour of driving time each way to work.

2. A 1,000 square foot house with a large backyard and a fireplace. Although it was under repair and torn up, it was situated on a beautiful street with large, manicured front lawns. The hardwood floors were being refinished.

I had my eye on the large backyard. I could see the children, now two and five, running and playing in the yard when we were looking at it. My mind yelled, *"YES, YES, YES ... pick this one!"*

Well, you probably guessed which one Doug picked—the 500 square foot Alley House. I could understand his need; it was clean and ready to move into, and slightly less rent, but not very practical. The kitchen was so small that you couldn't stretch your arms across it without hitting the walls. That is saying something for my five-foot frame. There was a tiny area on the right side of the sink, enough for a dish rack. The rest of the area only had a refrigerator and a stove. No dishwasher. With no room for a real table, we used the kids' wooden picnic table, handmade by Grandpa, Doug's dad. Doug and I ate one leg in and one leg out of the table.

The act of submission was becoming a problem and an epic feat to maintain. My mind was screaming. I was trying desperately to trust God. But I wanted to shout ... *ARE YOU KIDDING*

ME, DOUG? THIS IS WHERE YOU ARE GOING TO STICK ME? But with a decision that defied reason, I was silent. Well, at least on the outside. On the inside, I was asking God why.

Really God? This is where you want me to live? I reminded God that He had me leave a very large, beautifully decorated, brand-new home for this teeny tiny Alley House.

But Lord, I will trust you. I don't understand what is happening now, but I will trust you. I believe that you don't take away from me without giving me something better.

I'm not sure why you put me in Coronado, on this side of the bridge? But I will believe you. I will follow Doug's lead. The Alley House it is.

Chapter 11
Miracle in Paradise

"Faith is the substance of things hoped for ..."
(Hebrews 11:1 NKJV)

THE BEAUTY OF CORONADO made daily morning walks encouraging and uplifting. It was so wonderful having Doug home, and as he adjusted to his new position, the children and I quickly settled into a comfortable routine. Having him home was what made being married to this amazing man a joy. It was wonderful to have family life again.

Six weeks into our bliss, and surprise... Well, NOT a surprise.

Doug came home with an announcement, "The SEAL Teams want me to go to Alaska and find a location for a winter warfare training center, and I will be gone for two months."

I couldn't help myself, "Again!" I blurted out... "I'm surprised it only took you six weeks to volunteer for something else. Really?"

All my training with the Lord in Virginia Beach was out the window with this testing.

While my head understood the decision, it didn't even make sense. After all, Doug was an elite trainer in winter warfare. He had trained with winter warfare specialists from Denmark, Sweden, Germany, Italy, and Canada. And he taught the Royal Marines in England for two years. It was this skill that made him stand out to me years earlier, when I picked him out on the ski slopes in North Carolina.

I don't know why I let this get to me, because I knew this SEAL TEAM wife cycle was on repeat. I was dropped off and would be left behind in the dismal Alley House. I would be forced to manage every crisis and daily grind by myself, in California, a place I resisted with every fiber of my being. But here we were again, and I was no better at handling this disappointment.

Just like that, he was gone. The size of our home did not matter when Doug was with us. We were happy. But with him gone? Being alone and separated from the other wives on the other side of the bridge made the move to California so much harder. At least I had my relationship with God; it helped carry me through.

I was desperate to find my place in this megalopolis of new beginnings.

My front-door neighbor, Salina, was a plain, thin, earthy woman who smelled of musk soap. She had two children, an eight-year-old boy and a six-year-old girl. We shared a garage, with the washer and dryer situated on either side of an imaginary line down the middle. I hadn't established friends yet, so when I was in a pinch, she didn't mind babysitting for me, and the children had great fun together. Her husband was a reporter for the LA Times, so she was home alone a lot.

One day, I left the kids with Salina and went to hear Marilyn Hickey speak. She is a television evangelist whom I often watched in Virginia Beach. Now she was speaking at a stadium in San Diego. I loved listening to her television program and was excited to see her in person.

I didn't have a hard time navigating the city or being out alone at night. I thought I was early enough, but to my surprise, the meeting was full, and I had to sit slightly towards the back. The stage seemed so far away. She spoke about many encouraging things, but one thing stood out as particularly unusual to me.

She said, "Take out your wallet. Now speak to your wallet. You big fat billfold, you are full of blessings. Start creating it, start speaking to it by faith. Read the word and talk about the word of God, it has tremendous power. Miraculous things happen; speak to your bank account: You are full."

At the end, Marilyn introduced a couple of pastors from her church, who were planting a church in San Diego. Oh, what a joy that was to my heart. This was perfect for me. My spirit was stirred, and I knew I needed to seek out the new church.

On the first Sunday, only about fifty people came. But there were gifts in that room for me. It was there that I connected with some women of great faith. I knew I had found my support group. In that moment, I knew I was where God planned for me to be, despite my complaints.

My children loved Sunday School and the projects they got to do. As they felt joy, my feelings of loneliness were pushed aside, and I settled in with this great group of Christians who were embracing me.

I was praying for help with our finances as money was tight. And just like that, God provided a job babysitting Joan's baby boy. Joan was a lawyer with beautiful, dark hair. She was tiny, a little quirky, and had a lot of energy, which was manifested in her fast talking. Her son, Eric, was twelve months old and full of life, like his mama.

My children thought it was terrific to have a baby in the house, and Eric was such an easy child to care for. Joan loved that her son was so loved, and I was paid well. She would drop him off in the morning, and I could keep my morning prayer as the children slept. She then picked him up at night. It was such a blessing to our family that we didn't have to go anywhere; Eric fit in so neatly.

God indeed was supplying all my needs according to His riches in Christ Jesus, as it says in Philippians 4:19. I had a great church, community, and income.

I taught my own children financial responsibility by having them take care of Eric's needs and then paying them for it. Eric became part of our family and added so much joy and laughter. He was like one of my own, going everywhere with us. We regularly visited the library, the grocery store, and the park.

Beach days and pool days were rotated. The best part of living here was the beautiful weather. Every day we wore shorts.

Another blessing I received was from a church friend, Eileen, who gave me six tapes titled *"Grace, Grace, and More Grace"* by Joyce Meyer.

Joyce was little known back in those days, but wow, the timing was impeccable. They were just what I needed to overcome the feelings of abandonment and not being enough.

Joyce's message was powerful, laying out life-changing spiritual principles that gave me what I needed to stand and have hope in this season.

- I can't do anything on my own.
- When you need help, it is important to receive GRACE (and not try to earn it).
- He will never leave you or forsake you.
- Grace is the power to overcome bad habits, to make peace in relationships, and to bring you through testing victoriously.

Joyce shared her testimony of how difficult it was for her amazing husband to deal with her difficult ways. Of course, I did some self-reflection and began to see that it was not easy for Doug to deal with my quick-talking mouth when anger flared. Her message helped me develop compassion for Doug and showed me how I needed to reframe my perspective on my marriage.

I was inspired to hope. Again.

Several months after I had listened to those messages, Joyce stood in my tiny church. As I watched this powerhouse woman with a booming, deep voice, move swiftly in front of the church, I was inspired. Speaking with her afterward, I wanted to encourage her and thank her. I told her how her messages were inspirational, motivating, and had restored my hope!

I was now walking in God's grace, flourishing where I was living—the very place I refused to come to years before, and even a few months ago, was now growing on me. I started to feel like I fit in. At home, I found a painted stone I carried with me through so many moves— *"Bloom where you are planted."*

I thought of all the places I'd lived and felt the warmth of the Holy Spirit fill my heart. God was breaking the fallow or uncultivated ground of my soul and making it soft and rich. God was changing my heart. I feel fortunate to have lived in so many places and experienced so many things.

Doug was still in Adak, Alaska, 430 miles from Russia. But he would be home soon, and we would return to Virginia Beach. For now, I rejoiced in what God was doing.

Doug came home after two months, bursting with stories of his adventures in Alaska. I was thrilled to see him, as were the children. Even Eric got caught up in the excitement.

Now, we can spend the rest of the six months together. The hugs were so tight, and we were all clinging to him. So much peace came when he came home. I suppose for me, it was rest, as I didn't have to deal with everything alone now. The focus was on him and his love for taking the children to work. My children used the Navy SEAL obstacle course as their playground.

Suddenly, the fire of excitement was doused with reality. I listened closely to Doug's proposed change of plans to stay in California. This time, I was determined to keep quiet. My trip down despair lane was brief. In a face-to-face duel between anger and obedience, obedience quickly prevailed. I reminded myself how far I had come in my surrendered posture. Thinking before I spoke was never my go-to response. What could I say? It seemed overwhelming to consider staying in a place we could not afford to live in.

You brought me here, God. You will provide. I lay this in your hands. I laid to rest my doubts with that prayer. Having practiced turning things over to God.

At dawn the next morning, I laced my shoes and headed for the beach. Time with God was what I needed most. My thoughts were engaged in a whole battle. I was questioning God, but not in the same way as before. This time, it was about how God would work out the details.

Each morning Doug was home, I walked the Pacific shoreline, prayerfully pursuing God's promises. As I continued to turn to God and trust the process, faith became a revelation. What I mean is, doubt would be so far removed from me that I had the faith to move mountains. These times walking in the cool of the day were such a beautifully reflective time.

I asked God, "Which house is mine?" I absolutely did not doubt that I had heard His promise in my heart, and I would not let go.

Meanwhile, our renters in Virginia Beach fell behind on their payments and trashed our home to boot. Doug and I discussed it, and though we didn't want to let go of the home, it seemed the prudent thing to do. It was an unpleasant thought to think about the destruction of our home. Now it was just a house. We decided to sell. It was time to cut the tie to Virginia.

With that letting-go process, my heart began to take pleasure in the idea that California was our new home. Indeed, I had a truly great community here. I was blessed and content. No ... I was excited and ready to settle here, and I knew God would provide us with a beautiful home. I was also praying for Salina to get a home, except she could afford a big, beautiful home, unlike me. The competition was fierce. She found her dream home, and I rejoiced.

I prayed, "Let me be next, Lord."

I knew it would be a miracle, but as I continued to read and confess God's promises, my faith grew, and I was there to see it through.

Several months later, sitting in the warmth of the summer day, I closed the book, having just finished reading *Your Miracle Source,* by Marilyn Hickey.

I prayed, *"Lord, your Word says you will provide for me."*

Twenty minutes later, my husband came in the back gate, excitedly proclaiming, "I just got $10,000!"

He had met with an old friend on the base who told him he was eligible for a bonus, but he had to request it. Doug immediately went to the Personnel Support Department to request it, and it was granted. We received it within a month. The money would be used to purchase our next home!

God's timing was evident. My faith increased again.

Chapter 12
God's Miracle Working Power

"Now to Him who is able to do exceedingly abundantly
above all that we ask or think,
according to the power that works inside of us."
(Ephesians 3:20 KJV)

OUR LIFE IN CALIFORNIA was becoming more than I could have ever imagined. I was still holding onto the idea of having that beautiful house. I reminded God that just in case He forgot, I didn't want to live in an Alley House anymore. I would like a home of my own.

I continued to do the things for which God had already given me revelation.

- Tithe ten percent of our earnings
- Create an atmosphere of blessing through praise.
- Pray His Word and His promises and exercise the principle of sowing and reaping.

I was obedient to what He had shown me, and I knew He would provide what I had been asking for.

Coronado Island, called "Emerald Island," just three miles long and one mile wide, was a desirable place to live. The houses were six feet apart. It had the highest number of admirals in a single town in the United States. Every home had a well-maintained lawn, and those winning the annual flower show competition displayed their ribbons proudly on their lawns. I loved the flowers, and I knew I would have a ribbon one day.

The neighborhood featured a diverse range of home styles. Definitely not "cookie-cutter" homes. They had stucco with clay tile roofs, mostly in tans and whites, accenting the island's cleanliness.

My current home in the Alley House was so close to the next house, with paper-thin walls that you could hear your neighbor sneeze. I could say, "God bless you," and they would reply, "Thank you." There was no privacy. The clanking of breakfast dishes disrupted my quiet morning. I continued to pray for a home.

Ray Goett was a Godsend—the only realtor who was willing to help us despite our income level.

The only loan we qualified for required twenty-five percent cash down at closing. Wow... and that was a LOT of money. Mortgage payments were high in 1985, with interest rates at thirteen percent, making purchasing a house unaffordable.

I was kicking myself for being so stubborn about not moving to the West Coast in 1982, when my household furniture was shipped from England to California. I could now see that God had plans for us in this state, even though I didn't understand that at the time. So, I went through forgiving myself over and over again. Now I know God is the redeemer of my mistakes, and He will fix this one, too.

Suddenly, a shift happened. Five houses were listed for sale at once. Only one house was in our price range of $167,000. Doug was home, and we arrived at the property quickly. We were so excited, but our hopes sank when the door opened and we saw the yellow-and-orange matted shag carpet. Since I had been a realtor and Doug and I had already flipped a home together, we tried to look past what the eye could see.

We walked into the house, and the smell of fried foods lingered in the air. The blinds were closed, so the beauty of the southern exposure was not visible. I motioned to Doug to take his pocketknife and pry up the carpet to see what was under it. To our delight, it had beautiful, well-varnished hardwood floors.

We looked at each other and simultaneously said, "We'll take it."

I had prayed for a strong house, good bones, and a firm foundation because we wanted to build a second story someday, and we both saw that potential in this house.

However, after reading the contract, Doug started second-guessing everything and said, "Maybe we should wait." I slammed my hand down, looked him straight in the eyes, and firmly said, "Sign it." I was as surprised by my reaction as he was. Without hesitation, he signed the papers, and we immediately took them to the realtor.

Thanks to Doug's bonus, we had a good jump on the down payment, but we were only a fourth of the way there. My mom assisted in our miracle by helping soften my father's heart toward our need and by giving us a long-term loan. Slowly, the money was coming together. But we still needed more money.

Okay, God, where will we get the rest of the money? I continued to pray.

In addition to being short, the owner received another competing offer on the house, and subsequently, he increased the deposit. Again, the pressure was on.

Oh, God help here! What are you going to do? Is this going through? So many questions swirling in my mind.

Perhaps one of the greatest miracles was when a friend said that loaning us the money would help her. *I was stunned. Could this be happening?* She said the terms would give her more return than she could get from a bank. God moved on her heart to put together a plan with creative financing terms that would bless us both.

God showed us He is our miracle source. He used ordinary people to work in our miracles—providing something out of nothing. That was the ridiculous favor of God at work.

My prayers were answered. After fourteen months of eating off the children's picnic table, it was coming to an end. We would be moving out of the Alley House. Only God could have orchestrated His creative financing to come up with the twenty-five percent down payment!

> *"All things work together for good to them that love God."*
> **(Romans 8:28 KJV)**

Waiting on God was one of the hardest things to do, especially when you are so close to seeing

His blessings come to reality. Obedience taught me a lesson. Persistence in pursuing God and His plan was for my good.

When God moved, He moved fast, and just like that, we were out of the Alley House and into our new home with our belongings. It was easy to praise God now, and it was amazing to see what God had done.

I was elated and joyful beyond words to find homes for our things that had just been stuffed in corners and closets in the small Alley House. I wondered how we ever made room for it there. Now, my organizational skills, honed by many moves, went into turbo mode.

My mind easily moved past the ugly floor covering that clashed with our blue and mauve couches. Despite the outdated orange and yellow carpeting, I could see the vision of what it could be. As I unpacked and sorted our belongings into piles, I felt a sense of joy as I prepared our home. The bunk beds that Doug built were taken apart, and each child had their room—strawberry shortcake decorations for Alison's room and stars and rocket ships for Brandon.

We were thrilled to request our belongings be shipped to us from Virginia—finally! It would take another four weeks to reach us. But in the meantime, we would continue to eat off the children's picnic table.

I stand amazed when I look back on those fourteen months. The transitions that took place in my heart still astound me. I left Virginia Beach angry, doubting, and broken. The tiny house season and Doug leaving again tested me to my core. But God took me from resistance to revelation. Though it was the last place on earth I ever wanted to be, I discovered more blessings than I could contain. In hindsight, I wasted so much energy fighting what God was forming.

But now I get to stand on this side of victory and see the excellent work He has done in me.

We moved in just in time for a wonderful Christmas. Doug was home, and we enjoyed our time together. A fresh Christmas tree was brought into the house, cut down by the lumberjack, Doug himself.

Each morning, I woke up with a heart of anticipation, eager to meet Jesus, the lover of my soul. On the days Doug was home, before he left for work, I would walk just three short blocks to the Pacific Ocean. A simple "I'm here, God," was my greeting as I gazed out at the iconic Point Loma, taking in the stunning coastal view. Then, I'd climb over the boulders to the sand, where the fine grains stuck to my skin like glue, their golden shimmer dancing in the sunlight. The vastness of the ocean and the endless horizon stirred something deep within me. As I breathed in the salty air, I felt God's presence in a way that overwhelmed my soul. He had chosen this place for me. It was so much better than anything I could have dreamed.

This daily ritual turned my connection with God into something tangible. The rhythm of the waves and the serenity of the moment were a revered experience that refreshed my soul. With each step, I felt the weight of my worries lift as I surrendered them to Almighty God. I walked briskly three miles round trip, returning home just in time for Doug to leave for work—my morning routine completed in less than fifty minutes.

Back in the quiet of my home, I would sit to read my bible. It was in this stillness that I received a vision: a captured rabbit struggling inside a bag, trying to escape. Yet, the one holding the bag was taking the rabbit to freedom. In that moment, I realized I, too, was being released—to see the goodness of the Lord in the land of the living. No longer trapped in my own thoughts, I was free.

God's Provision for Healing

God truly thinks of everything. Our house was just around the corner from a Presbyterian elementary school, and Alison was awarded a scholarship to attend. She looked so sweet in her uniform; her long blonde ponytail bounced as we walked to school each morning. She was happy—and I was grateful. Especially when we met her first-grade teacher, Mrs. Methvin, a warm, broad-shouldered woman with dark hair and a gentle smile. She was a reading specialist who immediately recognized Alison's learning struggles and stepped in with wisdom and grace.

Alison couldn't spell a simple three-letter word. Mrs. Methvin introduced a multi-sensory learning strategy—spelling with thick crayons on index cards, using touch, sight, sound, and voice. Alison traced each letter with her finger, saying the word out loud. It was brilliant but also hard, frustrating, and exhausting for her. She knew she was different.

"I'm so stupid," she cried.

My heart would shatter over her words. I knew that pain because it had been like my own. And now, I was watching it play out in my daughter's life. Yet I was helpless to stop it—no mother wants to see her child suffer, and I didn't know how to soothe her.

Mrs. Methvin then referred us to a specialist in Los Angeles, so we went—nervous, prayerful, but hopeful. Hours of tests followed—visual tracking, audio processing, speech assessments, diagrams, and memory drills. They were so thorough with their testing. My hope grew with every evaluation, but fear was never far behind.

The results came in. Though her vision was fine, the specialist explained, the signals got lost as they traveled through the gray matter of Alison's brain. The retrieval process was blocked—her brain couldn't locate where the information had been stored. It was as if she had never seen it before. My mind reeled. *What? How? Why?* This diagnosis was inconceivable. I was stunned.

But God wasn't finished with Alison. They prescribed daily exercises to stimulate brain function and promote outward movement of gray matter, improving signal flow. After months of dedication, frustration, and many tears, we saw improvement. Alison was beginning to thrive. And although Doug was often gone, he was home when it mattered most, helping me overcome this diagnosis for our precious daughter. He helped with the daily drills—eye-hand coordination, bean bag tossing, and memory games. It wasn't easy, forty-five minutes a day of exhausting effort for this little girl, already struggling to believe she was normal. But slowly, her confidence grew. Her learning flourished. Her self-image began to heal as she gained strength in her learning skills.

And then I realized, beside the other blessings we had received, the greatest of all was Alison receiving the diagnosis that would open the door to her healing and recovery...this was why God brought us to California.

Once again, Doug did another winter warfare training. This time it was in Kodiak, Alaska, for three months. This was the third year Doug had been gone for the winter. The best thing about California winters is that they are so much fun, and we were able to do all the outdoor activities with the beautiful weather. With Alison in school and Brandon in preschool, I spent my days doing all the things you can't do with children around.

I was anxiously awaiting my husband's return, counting the days, like all SEAL Team wives do. On the day of his return, the house was spotless, and everyone was dressed in a new outfit. Excited to see Doug, we headed to the SEAL team compound to wait for the team to come walking through the doors. All the wives were congregating in the parking lot, wondering what was causing the delay with their husbands behind the closed doors. The children were running around, ecstatic to see their daddies.

Only a few moments passed when the men walked through the doors and were overwhelmed by the children clamoring to be held. Our relief at being together as a family was a release of tension, and we were met with an abundance of hugs and kisses. Once we were finally home, the house was filled with so much laughter and happiness—constant activity and surprises of what each new day would hold.

The Naval Special Warfare Group had been looking for a site for a winter warfare training camp for three years now and was getting the funding together. Not that I should have been surprised, but I was totally shocked when only five days later, Doug said, "The teams want me to return to Alaska next year. They're considering making Kodiak the permanent winter warfare site." Following Doug's encouragement and expertise, they selected Kodiak, Alaska, as the ideal training site. It was chosen because they would be taking over an old government-owned base.

The air grew thick with the words that shattered my heart. Then he added, "I told them NO—NOT without my family."

My breath caught in my chest. *I was glad Doug wanted to be with us—but wait ... Alaska?* The words were barely sinking in, and my mind started racing: *"Here we go again! This has got to stop. I am happy here. I just got settled."*

"You mean you want us to move to Alaska?" I laughed. "That's the funniest thing I've ever heard!" This time, trying to force a chuckle, but the reality of his words was creeping in.

The expression on his face was telling the familiar reality.

ALASKA, MOVE TO ALASKA?!

Epilogue

The truth is: surrender is a daily choice. Every morning, I still surrender my will, my fears, my desires to the One who is always faithful.

In knowing God, I learned to live in His abundance, His grace, His provision, His purpose, and His peace.

If He can do this in me, He can do it for you, too.

Acknowledgments

Thank You, God, for seeing me and drawing me closer to You. You have carried me through perilous times, and Your love and character are infinite. In the arms of Jesus, I have found true freedom, and I thank you for Your unshakeable love. Holy Spirit, thank you for leading and guiding my steps into the truth, and for continually refreshing and restoring my soul. You are constantly at work on and inside of me. You will never leave me or forsake me. You are steadfast in keeping me.

My husband Joe, whose loving support has allowed me to spend countless hours laboring over this masterpiece. He graciously allowed me to participate in the early morning Warrior Writer classes. His steadfast love and support overwhelm me.

Missy Maxwell Worton, my writing coach, her encouragement and instruction come from the heart of God. Her nuggets of wisdom aspire me to go higher, fully following God's call on my life. Her commitment to excellence and her pursuit of the Kingdom of God have given me wings; I will never be the same.

To Donna Bess: Thank you for your editing, organization, and constant encouragement, which helped move this book forward. Your support was a transformative journey that changed me forever. I have learned to be a wordsmith.

To my Warrior Writer classmates, your insights on this journey have been inspiring. We became a family of support and encouragement.

Light Warrior Publishing, thank you for answering the call to establish a God-honoring publishing company.

About the Author

Patti Oliver is a Bible Teacher, author, and speaker who is passionate about helping women embrace their role as daughters of the King. With twenty-four years experience as an ordained minister, Patti draws from  her rich life experiences to teach in small groups and on radio and television. She takes great joy in helping women discover how to live victorious, overcoming lives through faith and the power of God's word.

She is happily married to Joe Oliver, and together they run PnJ Oliver Enterprises LLC, a handyman service. They reside in Destin, Florida, and enjoy all the outdoor activities the Sunshine State offers. Patti has four adult children and one granddaughter.

Facebook- pattioliverauthor
Instagram - pattioauthor
TikTok - @pattioauthor
Threads - pattioauthor
LinkedIn Patti (Young) Oliver

www.pattioliver.com

APPENDIX

[1] https://www.merriam-webster.com/dictionary/insanity

[2] https://staff.ncsy.org/education/material/pxRD6HOLRu/the-elephant-rope/#:

[3] https://www.kuh.ku.edu.tr/mayo-clinic-care-network/mayo-clinic-health-information-library/diseases-conditions/broken-heart-syndrome?utm_source=chatgpt.com

4 Capps, Annette. *Quantum Faith* (Tulsa, OK: Capps Publishing, 2001 pp. 22).

Resources

Kenneth Hagin, *The Authority of the Believer*

Kenneth Hagin, *Healing Scriptures*

Kenneth Hagin, *Words*

Kenneth Hagin, *In Him*

Joyce Meyers, *Grace, Grace, and more Grace*— Digital Teaching Series from Joycemeyer.org

Marilyn Hickey, *Your Miracle Source*

Dr. Caroline Leaf, *Who Switched Off My Brain*

www.ingramcontent.com/pod-product-compliance
Lightning Source LLC
Chambersburg PA
CBHW071748120626
46550CB00002B/706